The Train Back

A Search for Parents

LEILA BERG

AND

PAT CHAPMAN

With an Introduction by
Dr R. H. V. Ollendorff

ALLEN LANE THE PENGUIN PRESS

Contents

You may have been taught to call me by the name of a poet, but I am no more of a poet than you are. I am no more of a writer of songs than you are, no better singer. The only story that I have tried to write has been you. I never wrote a ballad nor a story neither one that told me all there is to tell about you. You are the poet and your everyday talk is our best poem by our best poet. All I am is just a sort of clerk and climate tester, and my workshop is the sidewalk, your street and your field, your highway and your buildings. I am nothing more nor less than a photographer without a camera. So let me call you the poet and you the singer, because you will read this with more song in your voice than I will.

WOODY GUTHRIE

Introduction

by Dr R. H. V. Ollendorff

From time to time the world of the intellectual, the scientist, the doctor is shaken up by the appearance of an original, unsophisticated script in which an unlearned, unprofessional person reveals in depth the background of his or her life. Such a document reveals to an unprecedented extent the gap between a sick society and an individual, and the very complex interaction which takes place between them.

The success of the sociologists or the psychiatrists who try to trace such interrelations depends greatly on the length and intensity of their own personal experience. But, even with some experience, they very often fail to get into their stride, because only people whose entire life has been exposed to the abrasive and toxic aspects of our sick society can give a true account of the final outcome. It has indeed often been a deadly encounter.

The re-editing and translation of causative experiences into professional jargon often obfuscates the issues involved. Many of us have learned to love and appreciate not only the literary merit but the depth of insight of Dostoyevsky. The psychological, the psychiatric, even the sociological probings of *The Idiot* or *The Brothers Karamazov* go far deeper than Freud. And it is very possible that Dostoyevsky will be understood and loved and used as an irreplaceable instrument of teaching many decades, if not centuries, after Freud and similar schools have been revised out of existence.

I keep in my library, as a *memento mori*, a German text-book of tropical medicine. At the turn of the century this book pronounced ultimate wisdom in this very controversial field. Today the basic theory of every one of these simple diseases has been totally revised. All that remains is the pomposity with which the ultimate truth was wrongly proclaimed.

There are two ways of participating in one's own and others' experiences. There is the emotional involvement of the writer who dips into the foundations of his own experience, or uses the wisely observed fates of others, and there is the intellectual's experimental documentation of repeated observations leading to an objective assessment.

One can make no rigid judgement as to which of these methods gives a greater depth of appraisal. Each has its own strength. But the intellectual is prone to repress, to a tragic extent, his or her emotional involvement, so that this repression becomes a source of falsification of the observed material. And needless to say, the opposite is true – that emotional involvement without systematic observation, and the building up of well-documented records, can lead and does lead to sweeping generalization, which in turn leads the emotionally determined into the darkest of blind alleys. The ideal would clearly be intelligent flexibility. When people have been emotionally short-changed in childhood there is no point in giving them a very clever theoretical explanation of the difficulties that now keep turning up in their lives, nor is there any point in relying on drugs. What they need is love, warmth, friendship. Faced with Pat Chapman's down-to-earth description, it is clear that our emotional empathy must play a much greater part than the sociological–psychiatrical evaluations.

In this book Pat Chapman shows by the record of her experiences how the impact of a sick society often destroys not only one person, but carries over into the next generation.

Although Pat, the woman and mother, was exposed to cruelty, injustice, lovelessness, abuse of sex as an aggressive weapon instead of an instrument of loving and care, she somehow still managed to integrate into life, into motherhood which she fulfilled to the best of her potential. But nevertheless the same sickness of our society fell on the boy Richi, who in some way was already weakened by the traumata which befell his mother.

There are often situations in one's own life which give one an inevitable empathy for others whose experience echoes it. For many months, in 1934, I was in a German jail, and for some days I shared a cell with a young man, Hahn, who was condemned to death on a trumped-up charge of political murder. He was mentally dying every second in those days we spent together in our cell, and all his preoccupations circled round his forthcoming death and how to anticipate it. I smuggled some razor-blades into our cell, which he used, after I left for a concentration camp, to cut his wrists. Alas, he was found too early and repaired so that he could be given the full punishment. Soon afterwards, he was beheaded and his death was proclaimed officially on hoardings and billboards.

Since this episode, I have been unable to accept the death penalty – or the life sentence. And I still see and feel the terror of German fascism to be only the tip of the iceberg, whose veiled mass is a sick society with punitive measures of hatred, destruction and ignorance. It still appears to me that even in today's society these elements are taking the place of love and understanding, which are surely much more potent instruments of rehabilitation.

Before writing this introduction I thought it essential that I must first meet Pat and Richi. The professional intellectuals are prone to neglect those who have had the actual experience; they have been trained, in a mechanical way, to put their faith in the methods which circumscribe their way of thinking, and are cautious about everything beyond. Particularly are they suspicious of emotional involvement. Such detachment did not seem to me appropriate.

Both Pat and Richi are delightfully alive people, despite their catastrophes. Both are validly integrated into life; and one of the purposes of this book is to find a way to help Richi to complete this integration, by living in comparative freedom.

Psychiatry does not show up well in this story. Both Pat and Richi were seen by psychiatrists as round sausages to be programmed through square holes. The psychiatrists left them damaged regardless of whether they saw them or talked to them or not. The one exception was the loving, caring doctor, who sat the child Pat by the piano, and used the piano, and her arm on which he drummed, as an essential medium for her to express herself and to communicate.

I recently said, in a conference of the British Society for Social Responsibility in Science, that the most essential element of therapy is the person-to-person contact of patient and doctor. The trend of computer medicine is to interpolate techniques in both diagnosis and treatment. I expressed my feelings that this 'mechanization' is especially disastrous in psychiatry.

In a complex, sick society the sufferers need great understanding in their own social and economic setting. They need non-moralistic judgement on the disturbing features induced into them by this society. We are all moulded, twisted, by the frightening conflicts of primary sexual drives and the anti-sexual walls and anti-life barriers against which these drives bounce and ricochet. We are all structured in the image of our society. The psychiatrist must know all this, and he must love, care, support and always be 'on the patient's side' – just as earlier Homer Lane and now A. S. Neill demand that the parent and the teacher be 'on the child's side'.

But little of this understanding and acceptance came through to Pat and Richi. In Pat's case, quite clearly, a severe chorea or a meningitis or some such illness must have brought her into a hospital in childhood. This we learn when reading of her experiences with the good doctor, and other traces of memories of such happenings. The tragic result of behaviour disorder in childhood and adolescence stemming from this or similar illnesses was not registered at all in Pat's clashes with ruthless authority, or in the way her life was manipulated by all concerned in her earlier days. The heaped traumata of her youth must be seen and understood, if we are genuinely trying, with our professional training, to give her, and many thousands who suffer likewise and share her fate, the help needed.

Richi, son of a sick father and of a mother scarred deeply by her unaided struggle against shattering odds, intrinsically and extrinsically became exposed to the punitive machinery of our society. From adolescence onwards Richi never benefited from the psychiatric wisdom which surely had become available in his more formative years.

A schizophrenic father, a child brought up, with difficulty, by a mother alone – all the factors which we know to be important in social defectiveness came together; they were bound to make deep dents in the path of smooth maturation. Poverty, fear, terror, endless threats of violence were Richi's and Pat's personal lot. All this was augmented by the violence of the environment, where gangs, drugs, alcohol, delinquency constituted the daily background. A humane psychiatrist would have seen these factors clearly – not in order to drag down or belittle but in order to expand the lives of the Richis in our world.

We, that is Pat Chapman, her daughter Susie and myself, got underway to visit Richi.

We got into the train on a cold morning in January at Paddington Station.

The first pleasant surprise for me was meeting Susie, who is eight years and a few months, for the first time. She proved to be an enjoyable travelling companion. Children on trains always get moody, bored and demanding; they are full of 'Freud's disease', *'Eisenbahn Angst'* – railway anxiety – which Freud observed in himself and described so well.

Susie played very concentratedly with her doll, dressing her up with some colourful rags. Then we all had coffee, and played a serious game of catch-and-throw with the plastic coffee-cup covers. Susie is a well-adjusted, humorous, play-ful child, full of warmth and love, neither coy nor shy – the sort of child everyone immediately takes to.

Out in Gloucester – how depressing a west-country town can get on a cold January Sunday morning – an empty gloom emerged from every street, and even the half-closed hotel where we shared Coke, beers and Pat's sandwiches was on its last leg, as if tottering on the verge of a nervous breakdown.

Surprisingly the bus appeared on time and we trundled through the beautiful Brueghel landscape, in the heart of the Severn country. Then the bus stopped on the heights of a hill. We bundled out. We were nearing the climax of our expedition – meeting Richi. Pat and Susie were scanning the horizon excitedly, trying to differentiate Richi from the other figures. Then over the horizon swung a young man with a typical sailor's walk, free-rolling in his hips . . . and that was their Richi.

Susie protested at his long hair which was clearly a new image to her; but we were all soon settled, and the love and affection between Susie and Richi was so warm and deep that nobody could ever seriously accept Richi as someone who must remain an outcast in our society.

His is an open, friendly, fresh face which I found par-ticularly attractive, with a punched-in nose which strangely enough makes him rather more friendly than aggressive looking. He appeared to be very little marked by seven years in prison, and the friendly attitude of the prison officers and the inmates passing by showed a perfect adjustment with no loss of social integration.

There was not one atom of self-pity. He had not become institutionalized which, of course, is the greatest curse of prisons, forcing people to continue to be criminals in order to get 'home' again, burning the inmate far more deeply than a mental hospital.

An open-prison system, as against the traditional prison system, can be a very positive achievement, and with an adequate technique of rehabilitation and teaching it allows a good introduction into life. Freedom is a brilliant spur for the fulfilment of human aspiration.

Mother and son discussed this book. We all thought it wise for Richi to see the galley proofs before this visit. He responded as one would expect a young man to respond – with a load of embarrassment. And it became clear in our discussion that, as one could reasonably expect, he needed reassurance that all books like this are purpose-and-custom-built: in the case of *The Train Back* the impact of a sick society has to be illuminated as an explanation of how the behaviour of people is their personal reaction to the way they have been marked by hardship and sickness.

Richi, who has the natural intelligence of a man who can listen to others, grasped the point that *The Train Back* is intended not only to be a way to help him finish prison as early as possible, but also to show both Pat and Richi as prototypes of our society, and to evoke sympathy and understanding for the hundreds of thousands of others like them.

Mother and son together were just like mother and son under such circumstances everywhere in the world. After having the battle of *The Train Back* fought out, Richi claimed his independence from his mother, already in advance of the day of liberation, and stated firmly he would 'get his own place'. This was so much of a positive thing that there again the sanity and the love which rules their relationship showed up powerfully.

What remains to be said here is to elaborate a little on the concept of a sick society.

Orthodox psychiatry which has governed itself on the medical model, considering mental illness as part and parcel of medical illness, and giving therapy in the expectation that the illness will clear up as does pneumonia, is based on a system of psychological and physiological factors that are supposed to be present in 'normal' people, and superimposing this on pathological groups of signs and symptoms.

In an eclectic stratagem to enlarge the body of orthodox psychiatry, a certain number of psychoanalytical concepts have been grafted on to this.

The latest invasion has come from sociology, and again, after some fierce battles fought on the old ground of what arises from environment versus constitution, a lot of the sociological findings of recent years will be absorbed by psychiatry. This eclecticism is quite valid; the benefit derived from hundreds of thousands of such, often crude, physical treatments like electro-convulsive therapy will remain permissible for selective cases, while on the other hand the study of the total setting of a person will have to be evaluated before diagnosis, treatment and prognosis can be given.

It still however remains my conviction that some of the basic premises of psychiatry have to be re-thought.

In such a societal pattern as ours nobody can claim to be sane, healthy and normal. Nobody in this society can honestly say, 'I am sane, normal and healthy and I therefore have the right to declare my norms as absolute, and against which other people's behaviour is measured.' The shocking and traumatic childhood of Pat must have conditioned her to an extent which makes her adjustment in the present well-nigh a miracle. In the same way Richi has been inducted into circumstances which were bound to lead to catastrophe. I see everybody in this world of ours being measured against a spectrum of sickness, and the important thing, psychiatrically speaking, is to spot one's own make-up on this spectrum, on the one hand, and on the other to learn to accept oneself as one is, without moralistic judgement and loss of confidence in oneself.

This self-acceptance is a major therapeutic task and it is here that we find, surprisingly, both Pat and Richi win through.

This is in fact the glorious message of a book like *The Train Back* because, at the very end, we see Pat accepting herself as a mother, accepting herself as a damaged child who forgives her rigid old parents for unconsciously inflicting on her the terror which so marked her life, and so is able to give them love and affection after a break of many, many years. This acceptance allows her to be a splendid mother to her second child and to be a worker of social importance in a very tricky field, with enough love and warmth to work with children in an exemplary way.

Richi who is cherished and loved by his contemporaries, anywhere, is quite safely on the way to making a strong and meaningful return to life.

Both their sensitivities will ultimately help to build a less sick society.

So I come back to my statement that the documents of the emotionally involved are of very great importance. It is surely here that the strength of Leila Berg's work shows. It is absolutely necessary to have people who get totally immersed and involved in other persons, to draw out, with great sympathy and love, their self-description. Leila Berg is essentially a lover of human beings, and her participation in an emotionally openly declared pattern makes her contribution unique.

This book will be read a long, long time after all the psychiatric textbooks of today are out of fashion and forgotten.

PAT

Chapter One

I met Pat in Islington. Susie too. They caught my attention instantly because they were so unusual, unusual and yet absolutely representative.

Of course this is true of every one of us, looked at closely and with warm interest. But what was unusual about these two was that in this district of children in burnt-out houses with their stinking flooded 'areas' that harbour them like the traditional moat round an Englishman's castle, they seemed to be wrapped in mutual tenderness, like soft silk.

I have walked through this district many times. There are gaps in these terraces made by bombs that fell twenty-five years ago. The houses on either side are like smashed limbs with jagged bones protruding. On the front doorsteps, to greet you coming out or going in like the word of God greeted my parents, battered into unique curves like lavish praiseful cornucopias the dustbins spill their refuse for rats.

People live there. What does Authority think of people it treats in this contemptuous way? Does it expect them to grow up loving? How can one love in a place where the absence of savagery only means despair has killed it?

These were the questions I had often asked myself walking through this blasted country. Yet here were two people, loving. And the third person in their family trio was held for murder, and the three of them loved one another. It was not merely an alliance. There was anxiety there, I could sense that; but I felt that if the anxiety were removed, the love would flow even more strongly. How had this come about?

*

3

The first of the three I met was Pat. I met her at the nursery group. In one of the limpid squares that incongruously surround these raucous streets, in the basement kitchen of a large house, I was going to help Nancie, a social worker, and someone called Pat, to make a nursery school for 'given-up families'. Nancie I knew a little already; I liked her. Of Pat I knew nothing – only the blunt fact of Richard's conviction set out in print. As for little Susie I had not yet seen her.

If I seem to dwell long on the other children in this room it is because they were the setting. Their chaos was startling – not the chaos they were making outside themselves but the chaos within them. There was Molly, stinking appallingly, always wet, and incessantly whining, whose mother kept coming in to stop her doing anything, with words and actions of concern that was hostility hiding from itself. 'Don't do that – you'll kill yourself! . . . Don't play with beads. You'll swallow them and choke! . . . Don't paint. It'll poison you! . . .' And Kathy who poked into bags and pockets with a brittle untender impersonal curiosity and heard not a word you said. And big Tim, rejected by a mother who didn't want a boy, Tim backward by general agreement and scarce able to speak yet occasionally throwing up from the floor a broad grin that had a warm possibility of lovingness in it. (Tim had that hunched stance and shambling walk that instantly say backwardness; yet how far is it due to a primitive attempt to shield and protect one's innermost being – a palm curving round the guttering flame of a candle.) And Roger who endlessly washed dishes and if frustrated in it attacked instantly with anything to hand, Roger who at four believed he would only be accepted and only survive if he was useful . . . and four, five or six others.

There was no cohesion within these children. It was as if each personality had had a stone flung at it – a smashed mirror – and was flying out into separate jangling splinters.

4

Pat

When a healthy four-year-old runs joyously down the street, arms and legs shake wildly as if any moment they will fly off and hurtle through the air in all directions. With these children, neither healthy nor joyous, it was the very core of their personality that was in this frenzy of breaking free. I have seen this in children as young as a year old if their relationships are fearful enough – this frenetic chaos and blind panic to escape.

In the purposeless din I wrote their names up big, in coloured chalks. They were not interested. They were the first three- and four-year-olds I had met who were not interested in their names and turned away listlessly from them. I thought, how can children like this, without any interest or pride or delight in themselves, without any experience of cherishing, ever learn to read?

I put out an old teddy bear, a doll, a cot. No one was drawn to them. No one moved freely towards the games of being grown up, of going to work or cooking at home and tucking up the children in their bed and slyly, surreptitiously, energetically beating them. These 'babies' had no relevance nor interest nor release for them.

And they were so hungry. They came at one-thirty, so they should have had something to eat, but they were desperate for something to cram into themselves. Should we make a meal the focus point of the afternoon, we wondered, and build everything up from there ... their names on place mats, a job for everyone, talk, rituals, candles to light and to count and to blow out for real or make-believe birthdays, biscuits to arrange, colours to see, scents to smell, textures to feel and taste? So much could be built round this small vital desperate meal.

In the shattering noise I took Molly on my lap, showed her how to put conkers in and out of a cup, tried to retrieve my bag from unmischievous passionlessly experimenting Kathy, caught in mid-air by one leg the chair that hurtled murderously across the room from Roger's end as if we were in the Duchess's kitchen.

Then suddenly I was aware that a new element was in the room. I looked out of the corner of my eye. This was Susie. Quite unconscious of her uniqueness, she stood, calmly considering, at a table. She looked at a tiny doll's tea-set that Nan had captured for our use.

I filled a plastic jug with water, poured a very little into the teapot, and stood the jug beside her. She began to play. She said nothing. Perhaps she hummed softly to herself, but if she had done so in that cacophonous din no one would have heard. But gradually, drawn by this one completely absorbed child, the others broke out of their obsessed chaos, and gravely went and stood, one by one, at the table. Scarcely disturbing the air I put out more tiny cups, more little bowls, more jugs of water. Without a word being said, one by one each was playing, each was pouring, each delighting in a building of skill, each making a little creation. In the silence you could almost hear them grow.

Time passed – half an hour – one hour. Still they stood there, each separate, recognized, and self-accepted, each an individual rejoicing in his personal existence and his own personal exploration – yet at the same time all joined in a wonderful tranquil unity, all round the same table, all doing the same thing though separately, all calm and accepting each other's presence. And there was Roger too, drawn down for the first time from the mother-sized utilitarian sink to the play-sized teapot, relaxed and unafraid. No one had ordered this; they had grown into it of their own accord, naturally drawn.

Tentatively and very quietly I spoke for the first time. 'Roger. Perhaps Kathy would like you to give her a cup of tea.' He flashed a shy smile at me, without speaking, silently and concentratedly poured some water into a tiny cup, set it carefully on a saucer and handed it to Kathy, then silently smiled at me again, sealing the proceedings.

Nearly an hour and a half had passed. They had had nothing to eat or drink. But the children were so absorbed.. 'A little longer,' I whispered. Nan nodded. But what would happen when the two hours were up, and they went out into the street again and remembered their hunger. How had they gone on so long unfed?

I began to say, 'In a little while we'll clear these things and then you can have some *real* things to eat and drink.' No interest. In a minute or two I tried again. 'In five minutes it will be time for *real* tea.' No response. Nan wrinkled her brows. I said 'We'll clear away now and put out the orange juice and the buns and the grapes.' We took the tiny cups actually out of their hands. We laid the table, putting out the cakes and fruit that they normally grabbed with both hands before it came to rest on the table, thinking we were catering for their true needs. They sat there listless and motionless, all vitality gone. Ten minutes later, they went back to their mothers and we cleared the tea away untouched.

Well, I learned a lot from that piece of well-meaning clod-hopping. I should have left it to Susie. But who was Pat to have created Susie, unconscious Susie, love-serene?

I am not saying the children were not hungry. I think they were always hungry; even when they were fed, they were filled up like rag dolls with any old stuffing. But through Susie I learned that their hunger was much more basic than a need for food and drink, and when they had the tranquillity to choose, they chose to create; they chose to grow outwards, not to stuff inwards.

I had learned too how little, how unpardonably little, made a world of difference to these children. In this crowded kitchen, in this brief time, with this old discarded dolls' tea-set, they had begun to grow. The growth from that first frenzied distraction to that absorbed grace was so vast, and so little had brought it about.

And there was a third thing I learned from Susie. For some time I had thought that what children need are words – that children from such a background are starved of loving words that are good to listen to, of respectful and mutual discussion, of companionable conversation, of talking and listening and being listened to. I am still sure this is true. But beyond – just as beyond the hunger for food is the deeper hunger for growth-within-oneself – is the deeper need for tranquillity. From tranquillity comes the knowledge and acceptance of one's own identity. Then comes relationship with others, and the unspoken words that go with it. *Then* the sound grows, grows out of the relationship, that grew out of the self, that grew in quietude. In the quietude you can set the words and thoughts like flowers in a vase.

But who has quietude in this violent jagged district? How had Susie gained her quietude, that so gravely she offered to others . . . which came from the love that was so evident in her flowing inner grace? How had Pat given it to her, when her son was serving a life sentence for killing; and what had Richi given them both?

Later I was to see Susie by the stove in their Council flat, with the broken gas-lighter pressed to her face, 'phoning' Richi in prison. She wore a pink pill-box hat that Pat had found in a jumble sale. Pat had fastened a huge paper flower to the top of it, and draped a white veil all round. 'Richi darling,' Susie said into her 'telephone' with the enchanting coquetry of a three-year-old, 'do I look pretty? Do you like my hat?' She raised her shoulder, turned her head, and smoothed her veil. 'I love you, Richi,' she said into the gas-lighter. ('I keep sniffing at it,' Pat said to me in an aside, 'but it doesn't seem to leak.') 'I love you, Richi.'

Chapter Two

A week or so after I had met Susie, I left Pat tidying the kitchen while I slipped upstairs. The children had all gone, and Nancie, running a temperature, was lying down on her bed.

When I came back, Pat was pressed rigidly against the wall of the empty room, head back, back curved, moaning. 'Pat . . . what is it? Pat? . . .' I put one arm behind her head . . . and groped behind me with the other for a chair. Somehow I lowered her into it, and it was easier than I expected.

Then I stroked her bare arms below the rolled-up jersey, slowly and unhurriedly as one soothes a sobbing child to sleep. Either the touch restored her outline, her identity, or it suddenly faced her with unbearable anguish; or maybe these two were the same. She shivered, right through her body, violently. And then she began to scream. They were astonishing screams. They were very rich and endless. Peal after peal flew out almost visibly, like white doves from an illusionist. Continuous, inexplicable, they fluttered to roosting places on shelves, on the stove, on the window-frame, and surveyed us, quivering.

I put my arm round her and held her warmly against me. Gradually she stopped screaming. She began to cry. In a little while she dried her face and smiled a little, like an adult prepared to assume responsibilities.

'Pat?' I said softly, 'what happened to start that off? What did you feel when you were screaming like that? Were you afraid . . . or angry?'

At last she said, 'It was that doll. The broken one.'

And an expression flickered suddenly on her face that bothered me. It was the look of a child tiptoeing her tense

9

way through a shadowy, empty, cat-haunted alley, ready to run, a child seeing ghosts, or policemen . . . in a district like this they are the same.

I didn't need to press her.

Of her own decision and at her own pace she had begun to write down the story of her life. She said she was doing it to help Richi. It held me from its first sentence, and it continued to hold me long after I had finished reading.

MY MIND IS MADE UP

I

'Make me an offer,' that's what he said, and I thought 'What with?'

I wasn't very smart, well, not clever, and I didn't have any money, so what the hell was he talking about?

'Not money I want, my dear,' he said. 'Come with me and I will show you.'

'My Mum will be mad at me – I have to get a loaf for tea.'

Well, she was mad at me, which wasn't unusual. I didn't tell anyone and I didn't share the sweets I bought. I didn't share much, come to think of it, not thoughts or secrets – nothing. I did get a regular supply of sweets and I liked him. He was very nice and very posh and he was very kind.

I don't know why I didn't think I was wicked but I didn't – I don't think I had the brains. Either you know a thing is wicked and it scares hell out of you, or you don't – and I didn't. I think it was because I liked it, the sensation I mean. Anyway, I never thought about it afterwards; it just went clean out of my head.

Pat

My Dad was never very nice to me, he wasn't cruel, just
not nice, and I suppose that was why I didn't think it was
so awful what he did. Anyway, no one ever knew except
now, because I'm telling you. I can't think why you want
to know – still, I'm easy.

– Now, what did you say that for? You know you're not, so
why say it?

– I don't know. If you think someone knows, it's easier to
talk. That's all I mean.

– I know lots of things about you but it isn't what I know
that matters. It's what you know about yourself. Because
you can't live with them locked up inside you. And no one,
no one knows just how hard it is for you to live with yourself. So it's talk or bust and I say, talk. And if this is the only
way you can do it, then OK, do it this way.

– Well, if you think it's important – Me, I'm on top one
day and in the muck the next day. I don't make it like that,
it just happens.

– Well, tell me about yourself.

– There's nothing to tell, much. I like walking in the rain,
that's really something. I laugh just like a kid. I hold up
my face and let the rain splatter all over it. It just makes
me feel so happy. My little girl's just the same – she loves it,
too.

– Why do you think you like it?

– I don't know, I just like it, the feel of it. I like the wet
and the cold of it. Is that a good reason? It's the only one I
know.

– Do you like anything else?

– Oh, a million things! The sky, that can make you feel
good just looking at it. The sky. You might not believe this,
but sometimes it stops me wanting to die so much. It's
funny, me wanting to die, because I'm slaphappy really –
then suddenly it's all gone and I'm terrified and if it wasn't
for the rain or the sky or even the stars, I'd do it, you know,

just kill myself. Once I got like that and ended up in a mental hospital. What a laugh that was. I was worse in there. But I'll tell you about that later. You was asking me about something. Oh yes, what I like. Well, paintings and the river and walk abouts and churches. My little girl likes churches; you should just see how well she behaves. She tiptoes about and talks in a whisper. I like going into churches. I love the carved ceilings. I love St Clement Danes. You should go there. I talked to a lady in there who carves the Air Force badges. Thousands there are, set into the floor. And then look up at the ceiling – it's very beautiful.

– Can you paint?

– Me? No, I try but my paintings always turn out like my little girl's – she's three. I think, well, this can't be right. But it made me ill, so I don't do it now – paint, I mean.

– Tell me about your mother.

– I can't . . . I've forgotten her. I can't even remember what her face looks like. It is sad, but there you are. I think it went away, the memory of her, when I decided she didn't love me. I didn't say it just for nothing, things happened. Well, I suppose I made them happen. No, I didn't, they did just happen, and I said to myself, well, that's it, she doesn't love me and I can't bear it so I'll say from now on I haven't got a mother. And that's what I did, just said I haven't got anyone, and from that day to this I haven't seen or heard of them, not my parents or my brothers and sisters.

– How many brothers and sisters did you have?

– I had one brother and four sisters. I think parents should love their children, no matter what – you know, even when they are grown up, still say 'I love you', because they can never tell how grown up you are – you know, you can do grown-up things sometimes, real bad things, but you have to have someone else explain they're bad – well, someone like you, for instance. So maybe some people don't grow up. It's not easy to teach other people, smaller people, if you didn't grow up yourself.

– You can understand better now. But why wait so long to get help when you did the first thing? Why didn't you think, well, this can't be right, and tell someone?

– I told you. Because I forgot about it afterwards. I don't mean that exactly, but I forgot it was me that did it, that's all. I like looking at people, that's my trouble. I like looking at faces. Even on paintings, I look at the faces first. I wonder about them, what they do, what they think; I forget they can look back. Still, I don't want to start up a conversation. I'm just content to walk on and make up my own stories about them. But most times they're not. That's how it all started – I didn't see them as anyone I wanted to go with or anything, just as people to wonder about. I do it with you. I think, well, what's he after? What does he want to help me for? But then we get talking, and I want it to be closer still.

– I think you fall in love and then you want to show it. Why won't you admit you were in love with all of these men?

– One answer to that, I wasn't. Men are different when you're married to them, except for a few. I would want it to be perfect and it's not, because people aren't perfect, but it has to be for me or else I would rather be by myself, just me and my little girl. We have good times together and she knows I love her and I know she loves me.

– Do you ever regret having the baby?

– Over and over and over! You might be surprised I love her after me saying that. But I can't think why I don't want to go out drinking and dancing. I can be happy indoors just as well as out. I don't get fed up with my own company. I don't want to go out looking for a husband. But just now and again I get so restless that my head seems ready to burst apart. I see things that scare me stiff and I hear voices that I can't recognize and I just long to walk and walk and that's when I hate having her and that's when I start thinking, well, I might as well be dead. I turn over in the bed and cry my heart out, and if it wasn't for the sky or just a cloud sometimes that holds my attention, I'd be dead.

– Why don't you tell people about what you see?

– Don't ask me. If I tell them they just laugh. And in the morning I wake up feeling good and it just doesn't seem worth it.

– If I said it was a serious thing to see these things, would you be upset?

– It depends what you mean by serious. If you mean I might be insane, I would be very worried – I don't fancy going back to that hospital. I can't understand what it is these people are trying to say, why they come, I don't even recognize any of them, but I see them in colour too, and some of them are horrible – horrible – faces and blood and pus – and it worries me and I get sick in my stomach when I wake up.

– I think maybe it is things and people that have frightened you at some time, and that are still frightening you.

– Well, you should know. Me, I just want it to stop happening. Will they go away?

– I hope very much that they will. Maybe this will help, writing it all down, and maybe, too, it will help other people to know you better. You can't expect other people to know you if you always act as if you are always laughing at life.

– Well, I get the impression they don't care much. They would be hurt if they read that. I've got good friends and I love them all, but in the end I still seem to be cut off when I need them most. I suppose that's why I get a bit cynical.

– Why don't you like to show your feelings?

– Don't ask me. I should think I show them too much, if you ask me. Having sex is showing your feelings, isn't it?

– Well, it should be. But I don't think you think of anyone else when you're making love, and sex should be shared.

– Well, you've just told me I was in love with all the men

Pat

I took to bed. Now you say I only thought of myself. What do you mean?

– I mean you decided long ago if no one loved you, you would love yourself, and that's what you did. No matter who it was, they didn't mean a thing – you used them for your pleasure and in the morning you forgot them just like that.

– I don't want to be like that. I mean, it doesn't start out to be like that – something happens inside me and I hate them doing it, even though I want it, the sensation and relief, I still hate the fact that a man has to be part of it.

– You don't even know why, do you?

– Well, if I did, you can bet your life I wouldn't be telling all this to you. Go on then, you tell me why.

– It's all because of your nice, kind man who had you when you were ten. You just hate him, but you couldn't know it, and you never would have if you hadn't met me. When you can love someone else, then you will feel better. When you can have sex with a man and care what's happening to him, then I will say, well, here's a lucky man, because this girl's got so much love stored up inside that he won't have known what love is till now.

– Well, I don't want anyone. I got two kids and a lot of worrying to do for both of them, and there isn't a man born that could understand them, so we'll stay as we are, thanks very much.

– Tell me right from the beginning just how all this happened – right from the time you can remember. Just talk, and I'll listen.

Chapter Three

The ambiguity of it gave it a haunting poetic quality.

Yet I felt I must pin down the facts in order to present her life clearly, and in a way that would help Richi. I decided I would wait till Pat had finished writing, and then question her, and keep the two quite separate.

Later on, I found this was the only thing I could have done. For after Pat's manuscript ended, she moved on so fast that every week the Pat I met and talked to was a slightly different Pat. She grew, both backwards and forwards, from the Pat who held no memory of her mother to the Pat who six months later was to sink down beside her and say 'Remember Mum, remember?' and get her uncompromising answer, and accept it.

She gave me her next written instalment a week later.

– I was born in the country. Well, in a country town. I can't tell you much about it because I can't remember. I only remember from the day that man took me to his shed. Nothing seems to come to me about anything before that, so I'm afraid you'll just have to take it from there.

I went to school until I was fourteen. Then I went to work in a factory. They made big heavy uniforms and I was supposed to machine round the cuffs. I hated it, the noise, the girls, the forelady, everything about the job I hated. But I didn't tell anybody. I can't understand why. My mother didn't beat me. She wasn't cruel. So why couldn't I say 'Mum, I don't want to work there.'

Anyway, one day they gave me railway guards' jackets, and the forelady showed me what to do. When she left me I just machined round the sleeve and kept on machining even when my finger was right under the needle. I still kept it there and the needle went in and out of that same finger and people were screaming but I just sat there watching the needle go in and out until I fainted.

I didn't tell my mother even then. I just let her think they'd sacked me, which they had.

Well, all anyone could think of was housework, and I hated that too. I did housework for a teacher whose daughter went to school with me. It was all right when she was at home ill. I just spent the time in her bedroom watching her paint and reading her books, but other times I just waited for it to be over and I could run home.

Well, it didn't last long because I got sent away.

I stayed at my friend's house, and it was too late to go home, so I thought I'd just walk about until the morning. But I had never been out so late before. Everything is so still, your footsteps sound so loud! I liked it though, just being the only one up. Well, I wasn't, but when a street seems deserted you think you are the only one awake.

Anyway, I'm quite happy walking, and looking into shops, and looking at the sky. It had been raining and there were lots of clouds and everything was clean.

'Where do you think you're going?' Honestly, there he was. Before me out of nowhere. 'Just walking,' I said, as if it was quite normal – well, as a matter of fact I'd forgotten it wasn't.

'Do you realize it's four-thirty in the morning?'

I didn't fancy the time going so quickly. Well, it shook me. I felt tired then, as if him telling me the time made me realize how tired I was. I stood there. I didn't seem to have anything to say. I wasn't worried. I just thought he would say 'Get off home,' and carry on walking. But he didn't.

I don't know why I let him. I certainly never thought of such a thing when he said 'Come along with me', but it happened. Mind, I'm not blaming him. If I'd had any sense, I could have run, screamed, anything, but I didn't, and I suppose I've hated every copper since, but I never realized why till I talked it over with you.

So there I am living with my big sister, and very excited. It was at the seaside and I love the sea. Not that I see it very often, but just to see a picture of the sea makes me feel good.

She is married to an Italian, and he goes shares in a café, and I'm going to work in the café. So we move in and start getting it ready. It's a nice one, nicely decorated, everything's new, and I'm looking forward to it opening.

I sleep at the top of the house in a room by myself. My sister sleeps on the floor below. So does the other man.

I'm asleep, and then I wake up. And this other man, there he is. I just stare at him, and I am not so stupid now. I know, and I still do nothing. My sister is on the floor below, and he won't kill me if I shout, but I still do nothing. I don't know if I'm just a whore or what, but men just seem to expect me to move over.

This I don't understand, but you said keep talking, so that's what I'm doing.

Anyway, in the end I'm living there with this man, and my sister has moved out with her husband. But I certainly can't be expected to act like a wife. Not when you're only fifteen.

So I go out just walking, or down to the sea-front. And he gives me good hidings, and I can't understand why. I don't think it's any of his business.

In the end I stay out once too often, and then there is someone else with the same idea as the rest, and I'm in more trouble.

I know you said keep talking, but can I ask you something? Do you think some people are just born for trouble, because it just never seems to stay away from me for very long?

– I think that you just haven't the brains to do anything

to stop it happening. I don't mean to be unkind. I just want you to see that you've got to keep out of men's way.

– I don't get in their way. What do you want me to do, go into a nunnery? Anyway, I wouldn't like to be a nun, not even if they would have me. I don't believe people who have feelings can live like that. I think women who become nuns are women who don't like sex, you know, just never get that feeling. Otherwise their health would break down.

I was in a lot of homes run by church societies. They were terrible places. I could tell you a thing or two about them, but it doesn't matter.

I was telling you about this man. He took me home. Well, I couldn't go back where I was living – he would have belted me. So any port in a storm.

Well, I certainly got a surprise. There I was, very frightened I might tell you, and glad to see the street. I didn't know what was happening, but I knew it was bloody dangerous. I felt very cold, not outside but inside, and I was so depressed because I just couldn't understand why I let things like that happen. Just not to know why – it didn't make sense. But there just wasn't anyone I could turn to. You're fifteen, and you're a whore, and you just don't know why.

So then I'm in a home, and not very well if you know what I mean. And then it starts all over again, only it's not a man, it's a woman, and I don't <u>kn</u>ow what it is that's getting at me. I don't look very old, I'm not smart, I'm not beautiful, and I certainly don't act like I know about anything. But there's this sister giving me queer looks, and I'm feeling disturbed, and then if she doesn't look I feel restless and upset, and am naughty just so she'll look like that. I tried to commit suicide there. From there I went to several homes until I ended up in Borstal. But I want to ask you something first. Do you think I am insane?

– No, not insane. I don't think anyone is insane. I think

some people are born different. That's why I said before that you weren't born bad, just different.

– Well, I don't suppose you expect me to take that like a little lamb. What right has God got to pick and choose who he makes right and who he makes wrong? I've got lots of longings in me that I can never achieve. Things I know I could do. Writing, for one thing. And I've longed to act since I was a kid. I know inside of me I could have done it. There's other things too that I could appreciate. I can look at pictures, and they seem to stand outside the frame. The people seem so real, I want to reach out and touch their clothes, feel the cloth and talk to them. One day, I'm going to an art gallery and spend the whole day just looking at pictures, and I'm going to the Albert Hall and listen to a symphony concert. I love music – any kind – but most of all, Brahms and Beethoven and Mozart. When I listen to that kind of music I feel so peaceful, and I can't think of anything except what's in the music.

– Do you believe in God?

– I don't know what you mean by that question. I know I think a lot about him, worry a lot too. I'm frightened I might go to hell. I wouldn't ask for forgiveness, because I can't see any of my troubles are my fault. Once I thought he was in my bedroom, and I still wouldn't give in. I asked him why he did bad things, and why he didn't stop doing them. So if it was God, I suppose I've had it where he's concerned. But my kids, they don't deserve to go to hell. So I just have to believe if there is one he does forgive, or that will be another thing that will worry me till I'm sick. That worries me most, being mentally ill. I just couldn't take that, not any more.

– Why did you go into hospital?

– I couldn't tell you, I just don't know. I know I had never felt so happy. I was going to the swimming pool every day. It was very hot and I love to sunbathe, it's wonderful. The

20

sun makes you feel good just like the rain does. We were so happy my kid and me, just swimming and sunbathing every day. As if every day was the last, and I couldn't think of anything, only getting into the water and swimming. Water can be like a caress, and I just couldn't seem to get enough. Then one day I woke up and everything seemed different. I couldn't tell you why. It was just as if I knew that the pretending was all over, and I had to do something and I didn't know what. That's what I mean about friends not being much help. You can't make them see the fear inside you, and there is no way to make them, so there you are – friends all around, and yet still on your bloody own.

– Now what makes you say that?

– Well I had no way of contacting anyone. I was indoors with my little girl, and feeling incapable of reasoning anything out. It was as if my mind had turned itself off. I just couldn't see straight, and just this one thought running through my head 'get help', and I knew there was no one, no one I wanted. I think there should be an emergency system of some sort that people can just go to. One day I will have a phone. If I sell this, it's the first thing I'll get, just to feel reassured that if ever it happened again I could phone some friend and say 'I need you', and know they would just drop everything and come.

I made a mess of most things. I got married when I was twenty-four, and I had a baby the same year. I don't know why I got married. I wasn't pregnant, and I wasn't in love. I think I was just lonely and missing my family, even though I didn't ever think about them. I suppose I missed them.

It was hopeless from the start. Rows all the time, and I hate rows. I put up with anything rather than row. I always was like that. I let people push me around – I was angry, but inside me; I couldn't let it out. It was as if ever I did, it would be something too terrible to ever take back, as if I would be so violent it would never be over. I still feel like that now, and am just afraid ever to let my anger out. One day I will have it all out on myself. That's what frightens me, that all the anger stored up in me will well up and turn and tear me to pieces.

– Not if you let it out now. If you let it out now, you have a good chance of making it. Life will never be easy for you, you know that. You are too intense, too nymphomatic and too animalistic. You know this, if you will admit it to yourself and learn to live with it. You have other things that make up for it – warmth, and the best sense of humour I have ever met. You're fun to be with, and so alive! Don't throw all this away. Use it, the good and the bad of you, to make a better life for yourself. Don't be pushed into things you don't want. You can make it just on your own, and I know, if only you believe me, things are going to run for you in the future. So hang on.

– Proper little cheerful Charlie, you are! I don't mean to be rude – it's just my little joke. I don't know where I would be if we hadn't bumped into each other. I enjoy our walks and seeing places. It's good to have someone like you to explain about music and paintings and architecture. I've come to be interested in buildings since looking at them with you. It's more fun when you know its history, about the people who lived there, and then reading about it in a book. We were lucky to find those books so cheap. I like poetry. But it wouldn't sound right when I read it. But you seemed to make it live and flow – that's what it was like, a river flowing along, not jarring on your ear. I would like to find some more books when I can spare the money!

– Why don't you write poetry?

– Me? You must be joking! I might be able to knock up this, but it's only like talking. But poetry, that's different. I think a poet has usually suffered a lot. You know, had a hard life one way or another. Me, I've just been dead unlucky.

– I shouldn't think there can be anyone who has had it quite as hard as you, but there are certainly many people who would have gone under with the strain of it.

– Oh, you mean turned alcoholic? Well, there you are, I couldn't drink, could I? I turned to men instead. Sorry if it offends, but it's true. I just went out and went to bed with a man, any man. It wasn't that I said it or consciously thought it, but I just knew inside me that I would do it.

– Don't ever be sorry, because it's the only thing that has kept you sane all these years. You found your own safety valve, and it's as well you did. Why did you stay after your husband went away? You could have cut loose, made a new life for yourself.

– I can tell you in one word – Johnnie.

Chapter Four

Johnnie. Was this Richard, now in jail?

– He has been a bastard, Johnnie. I know it, he knows it, but he needed me and I needed him, and we couldn't hate each other. It didn't matter what I did or what he did, there holding us together was just one mass of love.

– Tell me about him.

– Mister, it would fill a book. I think I like him because he's kind. That sounds funny, seeing that he's in prison for killing, but it's true. I hate mean small people. You know, the kind of people who hurt your feelings when there is no need, when it would be just as easy to do a kind thing. That's why I like Johnnie. He loves people and he loves kids and old people. Everyone I meet asks me 'How's Johnnie? Give him my love.' He adores his sister, he calls her his princess. I always make sure she is really looking her best when I take her on a visit. He plays with her, and he worries too. 'Don't let her go out on her own. Don't let her talk to strange men.' The lectures he gives me on how to bring her up!

I said 'Don't tell me what to do. I brought you up, didn't I?' You should see that look he gives me. 'I don't know so much,' he says. 'I'm in here, aren't I, and for how long?' When he says that I freeze up inside, because although I know he's just being funny I know I helped put him there. I know it and there is nothing I can do, nothing. I feel sometimes I could beat my brains out with the shame of it, but I can't help myself – and in spite of everything he knows, and I know he knows, there is never a word of it spoken between us.

Pat

Sometimes when I'm laughing with him on the visit, I want to crash the table with my fists, and scream at him, 'Say it! Say that I am to blame! Let it out before it wells up out of you and destroys you! Hate me, you silly little bugger, hate me if it's only for a day, hate me and let yourself rest!'

Because, with the sentence he's got, that alone could drive him mad. Never mind what he's keeping from me about how he knows I was partly to blame.

– Johnnie never got in trouble with the police until he was sixteen or seventeen. Why do you think he went wrong?

– I have asked myself that question many times. He wasn't a mummy's boy, ever, but he did go to work, and he did get in at a regular time, and wasn't what anyone would call a trouble. I think it was a lot to do with the courts. They don't have much interest. The magistrates are old men, out of touch. They look half asleep, they sound half asleep, and so bored. Even their voices are bored. I wanted him put on probation. Still they're not interested, and it's 'You will pay a fine of . . . something or other', and 'You may step down.' Fine for Johnnie. He's laughing. But who pays the fine? Me. So many fines. And by this time he's decided that work and him just don't agree. I'm at my wits' end to find the money. It wasn't that he didn't mean to pay it back, but there was always someone hard up, someone who had done him a favour, and always someone just out who needed a place to stay at between. I was trapped. He can't say no, either. As bad as me he is.

Then it happens. After detention and Borstal, he's shot someone. I think I died a million times just waiting for the trial to start. He just couldn't seem to take it in. He used to worry me for new clothes, clean shirts, new shirts even. I felt as if it was some kind of crazy play we were all acting a part in, and that he would walk out of that court. I just imagined it would be like most of the other times at the magistrates' court, and that he really would walk out a free man. I can't understand.

That's why I didn't see it would never be like that. I must be backward or something. I should have known, and I didn't, and now I feel guilty. I should have done more, or seen that more was done for him. I can't ever get over that. It drives me into a fury – because apart from going up to prison every day on the visit, I did nothing.

Johnnie was no help. I used to say, 'Tell me what I can do.' But it was as if he had drawn apart from it too, and he would shrug his shoulders and say nothing. I cursed being poor, and not being able to go to someone and put down the money and say, 'There's the money! Now do whatever you have to!' If he had got a fair deal, I would not feel so sick inside. But he didn't. He got a dirty lousy deal. And it eats up my insides, trying to live with it, day in, day out.

– What do you think you can do to help him now?

– I am trying to influence people to make someone care, to make someone see that he has not got a sentence he can do.

You see, when someone goes to prison, they are thinking from the first day about the day they come out. It's got to be like that, or no man or woman could settle down to do their time. And that's what Johnnie can't do, because he doesn't know when he's coming out. It's no use people telling me or him what *may* happen. You've got to know what *will* happen.

He said, 'Mum, if they had said ten years, I would have done somersaults all round the place.' But not to know how long is killing him, and I think it's all wrong.

Maybe you think this is cold and calculating, that he should be too overcome with grief for having killed someone. Maybe you think I don't take it seriously enough, either. But when some get off, some get a couple of years, and some get what seems a whole lifetime, I can only see the injustice of it. And it clouds the other feelings that I should be feeling.

– Johnnie was in Borstal when you had your daughter. Was he very upset?

– I don't know. We have never ever talked about it. He wrote me a letter while I was in the hospital, and he said in it, 'You can do no wrong in my eyes. Keep the baby – don't give her away. She's my sister, and I have a right to her.' Well, there didn't seem any point in talking about it after a letter like that. I used to watch him with her, and wonder at first what he was really feeling. But now I don't worry. The love for her shines out of his eyes. And that's enough for me.

– Does she know her father?

– No. And she never will. It wasn't a love affair. It just happened. And I don't think she will lack any kind of love. Anyway, she may not always be here. I get a feeling sometimes that she just isn't here for long, and I go cold. I can't explain it. I don't know whether I'm psychic, I've never believed in that sort of thing, but every day the feeling grows stronger, and I think of Johnnie and what would happen to him, and I get desperate and I feel that I just couldn't take it and yet I know I must steel myself for anything just for Johnnie's sake. And when you're just staying alive for other people, it's not enough. That's why I want to write, so that I've got something of my own to stay alive for.

– I think you will make it. I've told you before you will. It won't be easy. You've got guts, though – more than most. It amazes me, all the beauty you see around you. Rain on a rose is beautiful to you, a duck on the water, and a man's face. Why do you see beauty in a man?

– I don't. It's just an illusion. But I do see strength, and that's all I envy them for, their strength. Other than that they've got nothing that I would ever want.

– Do you think you will ever want to sleep with a man again?

– I don't know. I don't think I ever did want to. In a way, it was just easier, if you see what I mean. I can live

27

alone, as I told you. I get annoyed with people who say, 'We must find you a husband.' I can find my own husband, thanks. Some women need a man always there. Me, I don't. I'm not domesticated. I hate any form of house-work. I would rather starve than earn extra money that way. I don't hanker after washing shirts for some man who treats me like a doormat, and only shows affection in the bed. I told you before, I could never settle for second best. I've tried it, and for me it doesn't work.

– Would you marry just to give your daughter a name?

– She's got one – mine. I went through hell-fire to keep her, and if she doesn't think it good enough, then I can't do any more. I love her, worry about her, need her, and want her. If every kid ever born into a normal family can feel that, then they're lucky. When she says 'Mummy, I love you, you're very nice', I feel I'm floating on a cloud. And when she says 'I don't love you', I worry until I can get out of her what I've done wrong. And to me, that's loving, and I feel easy.

– Why won't you tell her she hasn't got a daddy. Wouldn't that put your mind at rest?

– Yes it would, but the words stick in my throat, and I think of the dreams and pictures I see, and I think, well maybe I won't ever have to tell her. I wish I could go to someone and say 'Look what's all this about, who are these people I see. What do they want with me or from me?' But in the first place they think I'm having some sort of hallucination, and in the second place I don't know anyone qualified to explain it.

– I think you are psychic and I will tell you why. No one can answer my questions and not be. I am not a person, am I? You can't see me or touch me, and yet you walk with me, talk with me, and here you are telling me your story and answering my questions. Now only someone who is very sensitive can do that. You have a gift and you should use it. I will help you, and you will get even greater happiness from life. I say to you that you can foretell events, because I know you can; I have seen instances of this, and you have said to yourself after a certain event 'I saw it happen, but I thought I was going insane, that it was an hallucination.' They are not, it is just that you are almost a child in your outlook on life. I have never met anyone quite like you, you puzzle me and bewilder me. But most of all you make me very sad and very happy. I think you will always have this effect on people, because you cannot compromise, you cannot be inbetween. You can only reach the heights or the depths, and there is no inbetween.

– I don't know what you mean, but I just feel you are right. But you're wrong about one thing. I don't see you and I can't touch you, but I feel you. I know that I have had many occasions to be glad you were present.

– Well I feel a deep responsibility for you. I know that without help you cannot fight something that was brought on in you, and I feel people like you get a raw deal too. A seed is sown and it grows, and who has a right to punish what is no one's fault? Not even God, so don't worry about hell-fire and damnation, there is no such thing Do you think I would talk like this unless I was sure? Living is important, and making the most of life. You have hurt no one, only yourself, and that just for trying to grab a little happiness the only way open to you. I think you should write and go on writing. I think you should live and go on living, and if you want to, love and go on, right on loving.

Chapter Five

The next piece of manuscript Pat gave me started in the middle of a sentence.

Up to this point the manuscript had been written before I arrived on the scene. Pat had arranged with Nancie to type it for her, but Nancie had not had time, and now Pat was getting the chapters back. Perhaps a page had been lost, perhaps a chapter had been lost. Or perhaps her clenched cramped muscles poised to write only exploded into action when the first sentence in her mind was half over. Pat was bewildered when I asked her for the missing part. The 'alley' expression came into her eyes, so I left it alone. Much later she was to tell me she went into a trance when she was writing, and I don't think she meant it figuratively.

Besides, what followed the broken sentence had lost the astonishing candid clarity of the earlier part, that had made the shadows translucent. It had become less echoing, less painfully truthful; it was almost glib. Maybe I had come too suddenly on the scene, a stranger and a writer.*

I started to pin the poetry of her story down to facts.

'You start like a born writer,' I said.

'How did you come to start like that, and who is this person who asks you questions?'

At that time there was physical pain on Pat's face when she tried to define herself. She said slowly, 'I was sitting there with a pencil. And I suddenly heard someone say "Make me an offer." That's how the book began. It was as if he jogged my memory. That was what *the man* had said.'

'You mean, the man in your childhood?'

'Yes . . . And then I started to write. And this other

* The part after the break is printed as an Appendix.

person was asking me questions, and it was just like a conversation except that I was writing it down. The questions aren't me. Only the answers are me. I don't know what the questions will be before he says them.'

'Do you know anything about him?'

Pat thought. Then she said 'He's Dutch . . . And he's dead.'

'Dutch? Do you know any Dutch people?'

'No . . . But I know he's Dutch because he told me . . .'

'And the chap you were remembering about, back in your childhood, did he really say "Make me an offer"?'

She thought again. 'He didn't actually say "Make me an offer." Now that I'm grown up, I know that's what he *did*.

'Really he took me to buy some sweets . . .

'I was throwing a ball up against a wall. I was nine. He lived across the street. He had thick white hair, and he walked with a limp. He was a guard on the railway. He had a nice face and he was well respected by the neighbours – a quiet man. He had a wife, and two grown-up daughters. They were an old-fashioned family; they wore their hair in plaits round their head. And they had a garden and an allotment. We lived near Swindon. It was a railway town . . .'

We went through the complete manuscript in this way. I wrote and wrote till my fingers were knotted together scribbling as Pat talked. I rarely said anything, just put a question to get her started again, not raising my head from the paper, not stopping my scrawling, not reacting at all to what she said except that I never paused in my writing. It seemed to suit her; she did not find the silence disapproving. Perhaps the house helped – it's a friendly house – and the good meals – which Pat appreciates as she does many things she unfortunately doesn't get often; but mostly I think it was just being obviously, and warmly, liked.

'So this chap here,' I said, 'the one who met you at half

past four in the morning. Do you mean he was a police-man?'

'Yes.'

'What did he do to you?'

'He took me along this little lane . . .'

'And then?'

'He had sex with me . . . It went out into two roads, and he was signalling. There must have been another policeman at the end of it. Maybe he was telling him not to come, I don't know. And then after that he was still wanting to take me along to the police station as if I was silly and wouldn't say anything – just to say "I think she's run away from home", getting me into trouble like; and I was mad by this time.

'My brother and my father came to get me. When I realized they were sending for my father and brother I kept shouting out what he'd done to me, the policeman. And then everyone started shouting, and I knew they were going to get their side of it right. And the sergeant kept saying "If you did it, tell me." And he kept saying "I didn't do it – she's lying." And then that woman – I think she was the Inspector's wife – she slapped my face. And then I suppose they could see I wasn't going to say anything, so when my father and brother came they were all polite and nice . . .'

'And this next part – how did you come to stay with your sister?'

'Well, after this my mother she said "Would you like to stay with your sister in Bournemouth?" Well, I liked the sea . . .

'My room was an attic room. A short flight of stairs led up to it from their landing. The first night I arrived, this Frank came up to my room.

'I thought, why didn't my sister stop him? Because the stairs creaked – she must have known. So I waited for her to say something in the morning.

32

'But all she said was "We're going . . . You'll be all right here . . . We'll come for you."'

'But all that happened was, this man he took me down to live with him.'

'And then?'

'I just got fed up, living with him, staying in all the time. So I used to sleep out, in a boat under the tarpaulin. A policeman saw me. I told him "I live here."'

'In the end I ran away. And from there they sent me to different homes from fourteen to eighteen. Then I was out for about two years. Then I was in Borstal. And I got married within six months. And after eight months my husband was in hospital because he had schizophrenia.'

'And this bit – when you had "stayed out once too often", and this other man picked you up. Why were you frightened, and so glad to see the street?'

'Because I would have been seduced by more than one man. It was the whole house. That's what they were trying to do to me. But I screamed and woke up the landlady and they let me go.'

'And here – what do you mean, you were "not very well"? And what is happening between you and this woman?'

'Well, I had to go to a home in Devon. She was the matron. I wanted my mother very much, and when her letter came I thought it would say "I want you to come home", but she didn't say anything about coming home. And I was sat on the edge of the bath and I just screamed and screamed. And I don't remember anything until they broke the bathroom door in, and the matron was saying "You wicked girl! Why did you try to kill yourself!"'

'I drank poison. Leastways, I thought it was poison. Then I tied a stocking round my neck and tried to choke myself with my own power. She was very nice to me until I tried to kill myself. Perhaps she shouldn't have been out. She was out when it happened. And so she was angry. I dunno.

33

She pushed me away when I ran to her, and said "Get away from me!" I just liked her being nice.

'They kept me shut up until a lady arrived, and they said I would have to go with her as they couldn't let me stay at the home any longer.

'I thought I was going home to my mum. Well! I thought she must see how much I need her now.

'I didn't ask the lady, and she didn't tell me. She even stopped the car by the side of a wood and let me get out and pick wild flowers. It was lovely there – great tall trees, and the sun glinting through the leaves, and ferns and wild flowers. I forgot about trying to kill myself and whether I was going home. I started to think about living there, and making some kind of shelter. I just thought – "I'll live HERE!"

'The woman tooted, and it was time to go, so that was the end of that.

'We finally arrived at a hospital. I got scared when I first caught sight of it. It was old-looking and built of grey bricks, and looked gloomy in the half-light. I remember seeing a nurse standing in the porchway. I wanted to ask the woman why I was going to hospital, but the words wouldn't come out. I remember all the time she had a sort of smile on her face, and I thought "She doesn't even know I'm here, or else she doesn't even realize how frightened I am." I thought, "Is this her job? Doesn't it ever make her feel sad?"

'I was still clutching the flowers when I got out of the car, and I walked through the door with the nurse. Now of course I realize you can't try and kill yourself without landing yourself in a place like that. But that was the first time I had ever thought I'd do it.

'I stayed in this hospital for a few months. My mother came once, but we didn't say much to each other. I wanted to ask her, "Why don't you love me?" Because I loved her.

But the words still wouldn't come. I get like that when I'm upset, lost for words.

'I saw psychiatrists of course. But I didn't know then that they may have thought I was disturbed in my mind. I didn't want to live if my mum didn't want me. That's all.'

Chapter Six

Pat came whenever I asked her. I would open the door and there the two of them would be, red-cheeked from running all the way across the common.

'Here we are, hello . . . Susie, you haven't said hello to Harry. Go and find him and give him a kiss.'

'No, not this minute.' Susie was pouting and tired. 'I feel shy today. You find him and kiss him for me.'

But in a little while Susie was playing with dolls and teddies – none of those other children in the Islington group played like this; why did 'home' and 'family' have a meaning only for her? – and Pat was asking me where we were up to, and taking up the thread again.

This time she talked for a very long time without one word of prodding from me.

'My second journey to an unknown destination came one morning, and the same lady turned up to take me. We went all the way to Derbyshire, and it was a terrible place. I was cold, hungry, and bloody miserable.

'The woman pulled at this old-fashioned bell, and the door opened on a chain. I went into a dining-room. It was just long tables with forms. All I can remember is everything seemed a dirty brown.

'A girl brought my dinner on a rusty tray. It was cold and greasy, and I wanted to take it and smash it through the window, but I could only sit there and feel numb inside. Only inside me something was happening.

'Every day for nearly two years, I watched these so-called Christian women, with their grey veils and dresses and stockings and their praying and hymn-singing, working girls to death, bits of kids just like me, and living off the money they brought in. The Sisters – that's what they were called – always had a loaded table and a fire right up the chimney, while we were cold and hungry. I hated them. I hated myself for being such a fool and putting up with it.

'I remember once we were sat in the sewing-room after supper, and they missed one of the girls. I was sent with an older girl to look for her. We were passing the laundry when I heard it – a gurgling noise. I remember as I ran up the steps seeing something, a dark shape swinging just a little bit, in mid-air. I just froze to the spot, and I couldn't take my eyes off it. It was this girl, just a kid like me, and she had tried to hang herself. Nobody explained anything. Nobody told us anything. The police never came – nothing. Nobody comes to look over the place. Your parents just send you. And that's that.

'They said I was trying to go with a man. So they sent me somewhere else. I didn't really care, so long as it was somewhere different. They were Church Army homes, all of them. Seems like they had power over you and could send you anywhere.

'When I was in Herefordshire, I was playing up and all that. They said, "Come on. You're on a train." They put me on a train, and when I looked up the train was at Swindon and my father was on the platform. And I thought "I'm going home!"

'But he pushed me back in the carriage, and said "Don't get out! You're not coming home! I'm taking you somewhere else!"

'So I had to go on with him to Ealing. To a hostel. Nobody told me anything. I just had to do what they said.

'I was at the hostel about a week. Some girls were brought in late at night. Some were having babies and that. Some worked in the hostel. Some were out at work.

'Then they gave me a letter to take to this woman. She got people to do domestic work. She said, yes, I could go there. She said, "Do you like children?" She had a little boy, and he liked to have a story read to him before he went to bed. She said he'd understand my voice. The girl he'd had before, he didn't like, because she had a broad Irish accent and he couldn't understand her stories.

'There was the grandmother, and the husband and the wife, and the little boy. The husband kept making love to me, and so I ran away in the end.

'They kept sending me from one place to another. When they let me out, I used to go off and live rough. So they put me in again.

'I had four sisters and one brother. I didn't see any of them after I was fourteen, when I was first sent away.

'When I was in Borstal, I wrote a letter. I wrote to my youngest sister. But an older sister wrote back, and said they hadn't let her see the letter, and I wasn't to write to her.

'I got in Borstal because the war was on, and I was lodging with some woman. I was working in a factory, putting plums in tins. I got so fed up watching these plums going by, I began to put the plums in anywhere instead of grading them. And I had no money to pay the rent, so we started to raid a warehouse. Really it was to get money. But there were only chocolates and wine in the place, so in the end we forgot all about the money and ended up drinking the wines and eating the chocolates. And we got arrested. Two boys and another girl. The girl, it was her mum's house where I lived.

'That was the first time I was in a court with someone telling me why I was being sent away. Usually they just arrived, and took me.

'In Borstal, in one sense I was happy, because I knew I had to stay. But every now and then I got the urge to smash

38

the place up, and got a bread and water diet, and put in the punishment block.

'It was a time when they were starting this business of nine months and then you're on licence. Well, of course I'd been there much longer than that. So they more or less said, "You've got to go. That's all there is to it." Because they'd got the idea I was smashing things up because I wanted to stay there.

'The Governor just didn't have any idea. She tried. But she was completely out of touch with young people. But it was there I learned to read. I used to make excuses every Saturday afternoon, so I could stay in and read.

'They were called rooms, but as they were just the same as prison cells, I don't see why they called them rooms. Even if they did pleat the sheet, and put it round the bed instead of on top of it, and call it a valance. I wouldn't do it.

'It was in Aylesbury Prison, and you spent the first three months in a prison wing. And you could climb up, and look out of a tiny window.

'Some of the girls had a sense of humour, and we used to make up plays and have a bit of a laugh. But most of them thought I'd get them into trouble. I didn't take anything seriously, after all the hymn-singing and prayers I'd had since I was fourteen.

'I read Shakespeare, as much as I could understand. I spent all my time trying to understand the words and the rhythm of it. I was fascinated by it. Sunny afternoons we used to act it sometimes on the lawn, but no one would take it seriously but me; so it would end in a fiasco.

'They had a job to find anything for me to do. There was the sewing and machining of all the horrible uniforms and underwear we wore – thick stuff; the bras were made of it, too. And there was the laundry where we worked, the big heavy shoes, and the steam, and – we worked with the prisoners – the shouting and swearing.

'So in the end, they put me to carry coal. This was good, because it gave me more freedom. If it was a good screw, she'd let me go down the path on my own.

'And that was where I met the poor old ladies. They'd say to me (brightly) "*Good* morning!" And I'd say "*Good* morning!" And they'd say, "Aren't the daffodils lovely to-day!" And I'd think to myself, "What are these poor old ladies doing here?" And one day I found out. One had murdered her husband in his bath. One had chopped her husband up into little pieces. They used to titivate the Governor's garden, and bring their budgies there. And one day in church – I used to go to avoid a row – one of these dear old ladies poked me in the back, and said "You young girls! I don't know what the world's coming to!"

'I remember us all longing for the air-raid sirens to go at night-time, and us dragging our mattresses down from the top floor to the bottom floor. We liked the sirens to go, because the doors were open, and we were out again. But once you dragged your mattress into the cellar and put it beside the other girl's bed, they came in and locked the doors. So you wouldn't have stood much chance if there'd been an air-raid.

'I remember feeling sad when my brother-in-law was killed. They told me that, when they wrote to say "Don't write again."

'He was Italian, and he was repatriated, and his ship went down. I don't know why I felt sorry, because he'd left me with that man when I was fourteen. I don't know why I didn't run away from that man and tell my mother. I suppose I thought my mother and sister had arranged it, and she didn't really want me back. I suppose from the time I was old enough to think, I thought so.'

I was concerned only with getting clear what Pat had

already mentioned. But suddenly she said, 'I wanted to tell you. The other night, I remembered something – 'bout when I was little – and my big brother was . . . It was just as if I was little all over again, and my big brother was saying a nursery rhyme . . . and I was moving over the bed, and sort of trying to get away from him, and the wall stopped me from moving any further. And then I screamed. The rhyme was something about flowers. I can't remember. How does it go? About flowers. "Mary, Mary, quite contrary, how does your garden grow? With silver bells and cockle shells, and pretty maids all in a row." And then I screamed.

'And then I remember my mother and me . . . I was screwed up in an armchair, and my mother and sisters were white as death, and my father was coming down, and my brother went into this cupboard, and there was blood all over my brother, and I kept saying "What's he done! What's he done! Why is my Dad hitting him!"

'And then I didn't sleep in that bed any more.'

(I asked her how old she was, and she said, 'I must have been about seven or eight then, and he was seventeen or eighteen. I didn't really see much of him because he was older.')

'I didn't remember anything about this till the night before last, it was. I kind of relived it. I didn't remember. It didn't just come into my thoughts. I sort of relived it over again.

'I found myself saying, "Go away! Go away! Leave me alone! Don't do it!" And him saying, "Don't scream! Don't make a noise! 'Cos if you do, they'll think you're ill again, and send you away."' ('No, I don't remember that I was sent away before that,' she answered me.)

'I relived it. I was saying, "So that's what happened." And I was crying because I didn't want to know that's what happened. I didn't want to know.

'I can't say I really *remember* anything. But things just come back . . . like this . . . and like the railwayman. I can't really *remember* anything before Borstal and things immediately leading to that, except that every now and then something suddenly pops out of my memory, and I say, "Yes, that happened." It's like as if things are kind of being . . . bits of memory are being unleashed, you know?'

She looked very strained. I took a chance that the 'alley' look would come back.

'Pat,' I said, 'do you remember when I first met you . . . You said it was the doll that frightened you. Why was that?'

'That doll always disturbed me – ever since Richi was convicted. I don't know, I just think of Susan when I see that doll, and I just get frightened for Susan.'

'Describe this doll to me. How do you think of it?'

'It looks dead.'

'It's broken, isn't it?'

'Yes. Its face is very white, and its eyes . . . and I've just got this feeling Susie is going to die when she's still a little girl.'

Chapter Seven

They stayed overnight. Lying in bed together the next morning, Susie said 'You'll have to get yourself another baby, Mummy.'

'Oh will I, Sue? Why's that?'

'Because I'm growing a baby of my own, and it's going to pop out any minute now, and I'll be too busy looking after it to be your little baby any more.'

Pat was enchanted. She told us at breakfast-time, before we started the day's talking.

'Well, they'd given me all the bread and water they could, all the punishment they could, that the law allowed. So the Governor said, "Tell me what we can do with you." So I said "I'd like to work on the farm" – that's the Borstal farm.

'Then, one day when I came back from the farm, four o'clock or half past, everyone was locked in. So I said "Well, I don't know what's happened in the Borstal, but I've been on the farm!" And it was free time, when you could walk about, and talk.

'But they chased me, and threw me in. So I started to smash up. And they got two men to me. They threw me in, and hurt my shoulder – crushed it. They wrapped a wet blanket round me, and sort of frog-marched me. And I was terrified – I thought they'd suffocate me.

'The doctor came in every day, to see to my shoulder. Then they said they'd make a special concession, and let me go back to the farm. The day I got back, I ran away.

'I got over a fence, and another barbed wire fence, and kept running and running till I got to Kilburn. Some woman

43

gave me some money, and put me on a bus. I told her my brother was ill in London, and I didn't have any money for the fare, so she put me on a Green Line. And I walked about Marble Arch in my Borstal clothes, and nobody took any notice.

'I got into the pictures, and I saw a smashing film. It was *The Great Lie*, with Bette Davis. Then I walked about, looking at things and people, going down different streets and wondering where they led to.

'Then the dark came down. And I hadn't had anything to eat. Of course, I'd never really been out in the black-out. I kept falling over pavements. So I thought, this was no good; I'll have to go back. So I went up to a policeman. But he didn't want to know. He said, "Go on. On your way."

'So I went on, wandering about. And I kept seeing a slit of light, opening and closing. And then a van came along, and I saw they were carrying trays of food into this lighted door. And people were coming in and out. And at last I saw one of them was a policeman. And where d'you think I was? Outside a police ball!

'So he said, what was I doing there? And I said I just wanted something to eat. So he was quite nice. He took me in. I think they thought I was just a little kid.

'They were roaring with laughter. They were all with their wives in evening dresses. I said "Cor, who does she think she is!" and the policeman said "Watch it, lady. That's my wife."

'I ordered *everything* to eat – soup, sandwiches . . . I sat there in the warm, till they came with a police van and took me to Kilburn police station. And I was there about a week, waiting for the Borstal to come and fetch me.

'The first three days I wasn't even out of the cell – only where they let me wash. Then a policeman came into the cell, and he said, "The Borstal doesn't seem very eager to have you back. The policewoman is worried about you not getting air. She's willing to take you out into the yard to look at the horses, if you promise not to run away." I said "Thanks very much", fully intending to dart out of the door first chance I got. But I didn't. Because I was sick of running, and sick of looking for something. I don't know what I was looking for.

'When they brought me back from Kilburn they put me straight in the punishment block. Finally they let me go back on the farm, but they said it was only a matter of weeks. They wrote to my mother, and she said, no, she wouldn't have me back on any account. So they got in touch with these people who apparently had approached them about having someone on licence, on their smallholding. The Governor said this was someone who was willing to take me to live with them. They seemed very nice.

'When they came to see me, I was in the punishment block, and fed up. And they said to me, "Do you like horses?" Well, I love horses, but not to do anything with. And they said "Do you like cows?" Well, I'd never milked them . . .

'I was lonely, but I thought, "Well, I'll get used to it." It was beautiful country . . . miles and miles of it. Everywhere you looked there were beautiful views . . . there were rabbits and squirrels and wild strawberries . . .

'I was unhappy on this smallholding. This man had sex with me whenever he could. I didn't complain, because I was afraid I'd be sent back to Borstal. And anyway, I liked his wife – his wife was a marvellous person – and I was afraid it would upset her. So I let him, and kept quiet. Yes, it was enjoyable as a physical sensation, but when I was in bed by myself I used to cry.

'This man, he was very educated, the country gentleman type. He used to ride the hunt, and everyone looked up to him. He was very handsome.

'We were thrown together a lot, being in the smallholding together. It was six o'clock, and he was teaching me to milk. I was at the sink, filling a pail of water for the cows. And he just started.

'I think it's just me. They're like the age my father would have been. So you try to get it . . . And you didn't have any love from him, or you didn't think you had. So you must try to get any kind of love . . .

'I did my best to milk cows, but I was terrified. I remember one I put the chain around its neck, and tied its tail to a nail, and sat down to milk. Everything went fine till it plonked its foot in the pail. I got scared, and took the chain off its neck to drive it out. But I forgot the tail was still tied to the side of the stall. The poor thing nearly pulled the cowshed down on top of us. It was just as frightened as I was. Whenever I think of it, I laugh my head off.

'One day, I saw a calf born. I sat on the stump of a tree. It was freezing cold, but I was fascinated. I gently drove the cow up to the warm cowshed with her calf. He was reddish-brown with a creamy patch, and long spindly legs. Every now and then they would collapse and kind of sprawl out in all directions. It made me feel good, warm. I can't explain. But I cried a bit.

'I felt sure one day she'd suspect something, his wife. And I couldn't run away, because I was on licence, and they'd have clapped me straight back in the nick.

'I didn't want to marry the man. It was an escape. She could see I didn't want to. She begged me not to. She sat on the edge of the bath and she begged me. But I couldn't tell her why I had to.'

'And this chap you married, who was he?'

'They were Londoners, and had been evacuated to this farm, which had been left to them by this man's father. And he used to come down at week-ends.

'I used to go down past the farm-house. In a country place, anyone who goes by is news. And his mother saw me, and asked me who I was. And I told her I was working up at this big house.

'So she asked me to tea. And I thought, "That's good." Her son was there, and she said "See her back across the fields." In six months I was married . . . and I wasn't having a baby.'

'What was he like?'

'He was dominating to a degree of cruelty, and I was completely in his power. He stopped me having any friends.

'I got pregnant a month *after* I was married, and we came back to London before Richi was born.

'And he came home one night, and he said "Get ready", because he was going to take me to hospital. And in the hospital, he said something to the nurse. And she said to me, "Come along with me." And she took me to a room, and she told me my husband said he had a disease, and I was having this baby . . .

'I didn't know whether he really had it, or if he was trying to hurt me. When he was up in London, he said, and I was living with his mother in the country, he'd picked up a woman in Berners Street, and took her to his room.

'I cried. I was frightened of what it would do to the baby. I was cruel to him about it, but then he was cruel to me, kind of swishing it around as if I'd given it to him. And then I was nearly out of my mind, because I knew I hadn't been with anyone else.

'And I think then that's what he decided – that I'd given it to him. For a few days, he'd be ever so kind. And then he'd be ever so cruel for weeks on end. And then he just wouldn't let me go anywhere.

'Every time I went shopping, he accused me of going with men. If anyone came . . . just a young man . . . my friend's son, he was only twelve, he used to come to help me because I was ill when I was carrying Richard . . .

'When I was going to have the baby, he didn't even get up out of bed. And I didn't know anything about it, about the pains and that. I had to get up and get dressed, go and ask other people. And I was so fed up with it all, I didn't even bother to put on my wedding ring.

'I said to this woman– she was a neighbour – I said "I haven't brought my wedding ring." She said "We'll have to go back and get it!" I said "No, it doesn't matter. Bring it when you come, some time." She said "You can't go in a hospital and have a baby without a wedding ring!" I thought this was funny . . .

'Afterwards, I went back. And we only had one room.

'He didn't take much notice of Richi. He always seemed lost in his own thoughts. It got more and more difficult to live with him over the years.

'You can't just pick a man up and carry him to the doctor. I kept running to the doctor's, and begging him to come to the house. But of course he couldn't just come to the house.

'He'd swear blind I'd changed all the furniture round . . . And in the end, things start to go boom in your head. And because he's not shouting or worked up like you are, you begin to think it's you that's going mad. And he would take the back off the television set while it was going, to look for hidden microphones, he said. And he started to talk about having murdered someone and the police were looking for him.

'But he was holding a job down all this time. I dreaded six o'clock coming, and him coming home. If his firm had only seen me . . . I suppose they were doing their best. He wasn't really fit to do any work, and they were just covering up for him. But if only they'd talked to me. I just didn't know.

'It was years before I got him to a doctor. Then he started to talk about killing me, and how it wouldn't hurt and that. The doctor was giving me tablets to buck me up. I was crying a lot. And I found they'd keep me awake. So I started taking them to keep me awake.

'In the end, he did get to the doctor. The first three times, I didn't go in with him. He was a domineering man. He came out with eye drops and ear drops. We had weeks of that.

'But finally he did go. And they gave me a letter to Bart's. The doctor had had me running round to him half-way up the wall for six months, so he knew there must be something wrong. I suppose he talked to him about murders and so on, and then he was able to do it.

'I saw the secretary. And she read it, and said yes, and she wanted to make an appointment for two months ahead. Well, this had been going on for two years. I'd been locking the baby up to keep him safe. So of course I started to smash up the cups and that, they brought the coffee in. I couldn't go back to that for another two bloody months. So they called the doctors, and they said, would I go to the hospital in St Pancras. So I got in a car – once more – and went with them. I couldn't have cared less.

'The doctor there said "There's nothing wrong with you mentally. But you need a good rest. Will you stay here for a bit?" So I stayed.

'And the next day he came to see me. By that time I didn't want to see him any more. I suppose I was crying and hysterical. In a few minutes the doctor came over. And then he said, "I've only spoken a few words to this man, and I can see he's very ill." So after all that bloody time, they take him away and certify him – by a trick really. But you can't get anyone to help at the beginning, to save your sanity and your kid's sanity.

'All this time, Richi was with the next door neighbour. I was there about six weeks. I didn't need anything, except for someone to take this burden off my mind. It was too much for me to cope with.

'And even then, they tricked me. He was there for six months, and he seemed a lot better. I used to say to the nurses, "How is he?" And they said, "Oh, he's getting on fine." Then he started to talk about coming home. I asked the nurses. I thought they were giving me advice. They said he was better. To me, "better" meant "well". So he started coming home for week-ends. Then I discovered he'd been released "in my custody"!

'Well, I couldn't take the responsibility. Almost immediately he started bringing knives up into the bedroom. It started all over again.

'Richi was about eight. He started getting upset. I never told him what was wrong with his father, never have done to this day. I don't know whether anyone else has told him.

'I was in the house by myself with him.* I was still dominated by him, even though he was in hospital (just coming home for week-ends). I wrote to his family and asked if they would share the burden and have him sometimes for week-ends, but they never answered. They didn't want to know.

'I was trying to protect Richi from seeing his father like this . . . send him out to play . . .

'Then one day, I took him back, and we had to change buses at Finsbury Park. He had his case, and he had an electric razor in it with a long lead. While he was waiting, he said he was going to the toilet.

'I waited and waited, and he didn't come up. At last, I told the attendant, and he went down, and said "There isn't anyone there!" The police came, and rode me round and round the park at the back. I thought "We'll find him dead somewhere." I was in a terrible state. They said "We'd better give you a hot drink" . . . Then a phone call came through. He'd just returned to hospital.

'Then one day I said I couldn't stand it any more. "He can't come out!" So he stayed in for a few weeks.

'My brother-in-law – he lived downstairs – was getting

* Her husband.

worried. Then the hospital said, they'd got a wonder drug –
"Just see that he takes it while he's out, and he'll have a very
nice day."

'Well, we went to the pictures. And he kept getting up and
walking about, and I kept getting up and following him – I
didn't know what to do. When we got home, he fetched
knives and razors up to the bedroom and put them on top of
the wardrobe.

'I'd got Richi out of the way for the week-end. One
brother-in-law lived downstairs; they'd gone away. And
the other lived at New Cross.

'He was just smiling all the time. I tried not to take any
notice. I went to take the dog out. And when I came back,
the door was locked. I could hear a sound like a knife being
sharpened. He had a stone – he did carpentry a lot.

'I went to the man next door for help. But you can't
blame him. He had children of his own. I stopped a police
car that was coming up the street. The police burst the door
in, and wrapped a towel round his neck.

'By that time, he'd cut his throat with a razor and a knife.
There was blood all over the place. The police said to him,
"Why did you do it, son?" And he said "Because I've just
killed my wife. There she is lying there."'

Chapter Eight

'And that's the last time I've had him out. I know it's right not to have him out, but I feel guilty about it, you know.

'I couldn't even talk about Richi to him. He didn't even accept that he had Richi. He said his "wife and daughters" were dead in a fire. And then he stopped talking altogether.

'My doctor said he couldn't see the point of us both being ill, and advised me not to go any more. So I took his advice.

'But then I got a letter saying he was very ill. When I went, when I got nearer . . . I got so sick and vomiting. You can't go in and not see him. You feel for him. And you think it's terrible. At least, I do. And when I got to him, I didn't believe it was my husband. I called the nurse, and said "You've put me by the wrong man." But he said "No, it's your husband." I couldn't believe it. His arms were like matchsticks, his face all sunken in. He looked about sixty. I said to the nurse, "You're starving him!" But he said, he wouldn't take any food.

'I went as many days as I could. Sometimes I walked all the way* because I didn't have any money at the time. And then, I just stopped going.

'So then I just brought Richi up the best way I could. He had a sense of humour right from when he was a kid. He could always cheer you up.

'I never had any National Assistance – I didn't even know about National Assistance till Nancie came on the scene. But I had money from his firm – the union was so good. So we had some money. But of course, in the first years a lot of it went on taking things to hospital. And the union sent Richi

* From Islington to Barnet.

things at Christmas time. Richi wore his trousers out in no time, and his shoes. I tried to let him go places where other kids went. But all the time it cost money. I suppose I'd never really ate as I should, but I always tried to use the money for Richi. When the money stopped from the union, I went back to work.

'I worked in cafés, BBC canteen, and places like that. The money wasn't much good, because you had to pay for fares, and stockings – you had to keep yourself reasonably smart; so I was worse off really. People don't understand. And I didn't have any special friend. People I did sort of look on as friends kind of let me down in the end. It was all right when you were laughing and joking, but when you get depressed . . .

'When Richi was twelve, he didn't want to go to the pictures with me any more. He wanted to go with his mates. So I found myself just picking up men and having sex and going home to bed. Not for the money. Just a way of getting everything for a little while. I never wanted to see them again. I felt nothing was permanent, so there was no point. It was my own way of keeping my head above water. I had to go on living for Richi's sake.

'Then Richi left school. He was fourteen.

'He went to work in a printing firm, but he never liked it. He couldn't bear to be shut in. So he stuck it for a year. I thought, he'll get used to it. I encouraged him to go. But he was only a boy, and he was doing things like sweeping up, you know; so he left it. And then he had lots of odd jobs.

'Then when he was sixteen, he kind of stopped working altogether. At first, I didn't know he wasn't working. When he was sixteen, he got a job that he said he wanted – asphalting. He used to go out with boots and that. And one day, I saw him in Upper Street in the middle of the day. I couldn't understand it, because this is what he said he always wanted, working in the open air. This was outside the arcade, where the machines are. I had a talk with him.

'It was right bad luck, but the fellow who was the foreman was a fellow who could talk his head off, and he knew someone who knew his father, and he never stopped talking to Richi about his Dad. This bloke sort of took him under his wing, but he was ignorant. Richi said to me, "He keeps on about things Dad did." He didn't say much, but he said enough for me to know it was no use trying to make him go back.

'By then, I had a job in a shop, near home. The woman who owned the shop, my friend, lived opposite me. She saw Richi – he was supposed to be working – go into the house. She said to me, "Go in. Bring him to his senses. Throw him out!" I said "I can't do that to my own kid." She said, "Go on!" Well, I went. I felt sick. I shouted. He never answered back. He never has answered back.

'So he went. The first week he was away, he used to come round every day. I used to say, "You're not coming back till you go to work." He used to say, "It's all right, darling. I've only come round for a cup of tea." We wasn't bad friends. I couldn't hate him – it was no good.

'Then, on the Friday, he come round for the rent for the lady whose house he was living in. I said, "Where's the money you got from work? You said you were working." He said, "Oh, there was a mix-up with the wages." I said "All right. How much?" He said, "Three pounds." I said, "What kind of a room you got, then?" He said, "I'm sleeping on the woman's settee." I thought, "This is no good." But I remembered what the woman said, "Be firm with him." So I left it for another week. Then he came around for money the next week. So I said, "Come home. It's cheaper." So he came back, then.

'He was going in some café at that time. A few months after was the first time he got arrested – for fighting. They said he had an offensive weapon, because he had a thick belt round his jeans – they were the fashion then. That was the first time – he was seventeen – that he was in any trouble with the police.

'He got a fine. I wanted them to give him probation, so that he would be under somebody's guidance, and I would have someone behind me to back me up. But you don't get any sort of say. You can't get to anybody. Of course, I had to pay the fine. It was ridiculous.

'I don't suppose they ever knew or cared he hadn't a father. I had to go out to work to earn money, and it was shift work. I had to work on Sundays to get enough.

'And in spite of everything he was doing – and I was sad about it – I couldn't hate him. He was the kind of boy you couldn't hate. I don't suppose he could ever understand that it was him that was making me unhappy. I suppose really he'd got like me, very depressed and that. So if he saw me looking miserable, he'd say "What's the matter, darling? I'll make you a cup of tea. Cheer up." And he'd laugh and joke. He didn't seem to understand he was the cause of it. I don't say he was all the cause.

'He didn't care.* If he saw an old man and an old lady crossing the street, he'd carry their bags and stop the traffic. His mates would be behind, laughing, but he wouldn't care.

'I couldn't go to work myself what with him and everything else worrying me. So I stopped work too. And then there was no money coming in. So we existed on £3 19s 6d for a long, long time. That was off my husband's National Health thing.

'Then he got fined for driving away a car. The people opposite gave him a job, and they still ask after him. They liked him very much. It was marvellous really. I could look

---

* Meaning not he was callous, but the opposite – did what he spontaneously felt, was not put off by ridicule or anything else.

out of the window, and see him going to work. But unfortunately it was a small business, and they had to give him the sack.

'Then the next thing he did, I think he was eighteen. He got three months detention. So much has happened. I can't remember what that was for. I hoped they'd give him probation, and help him find a decent job.

'When he came out, he was more or less cattled, because nobody wants to give him a job when you've been away. He didn't get a job for ages.

'Then he got a job with a small firm. They were those models that they put in shops, and he had just to rub the legs and arms down with sandpaper. The man couldn't pay him a high wage. He was getting about eight pound a week. He used to come home covered with white powder, and all his eyes were sore. But he got on, and although he hated it he could still laugh and joke. And there were all sorts of people there, course, as they were people who couldn't get jobs anywhere else . . . Greeks and coloured people and old men . . . well, he thought they were old.

'He was working all right. And then he went out one night. Really, it was through me he went to this place. We was right up the wall. We didn't have any money. And I had some clothes this woman said she'd buy off me. And I let her buy the clothes, but she didn't bring the money back. So by Friday I was moaning, saying "Bloody woman!" So he said, "I'll go down to her, and ask her what she's done with the money."

'So he's met some boys down there . . . and they're standing in a group, talking. His mates are a little way behind him, and without Richi knowing, there's been some bumping with the coloured boy. So the next minute, a brick hit Richi on the side of the head. Richi looked a bit like this other chap from the back, and the coloured boy had run off and aimed a brick and hit Richi.

'I'll tell you it as I remember it, but somewhere it seems muddled. He chased this boy. And he had a paper-knife in his pocket. They say he stabbed him, but actually it only went in a little way and didn't even need stitches, and the case was dismissed.

'Going round the firm, talking to this man*, who was a very nice man . . . saying "Oh, he's fine" . . . well, through this man, Richi used to go to a boxing ring three times a week ('cos this man's mate helped with this boxing club) in a church hall.

'It was a great thing. Richi was just beginning not to have such late nights. This man liked working with rather wild boys, you know; he was doing a bloody good job – not talking religion, you know. But the vicar stopped him using the hall, because none of them were church-goers.

'The boys were well-behaved and under control, and they respected Jackie and he was doing some good. And I think if Richi had had just a few more weeks and a few more talks with this fellow, perhaps he'd have settled down. But it all fell through.

'He was sick, because it was a place where he didn't have to have money to get in. The man ran it on a shoe-string, used his own equipment and that. So he just drifted back to caffs.

'And then, you know, he started to go thieving. By then, he's nineteen, and your control over him has gone. I don't mean he was bad to me. He was just bad to himself.

'He got probation for something, finally. I don't remember what it was for. He had one first.† I could talk to him. Richi could talk to him. But suddenly, after about a fortnight, he had a change of probation officer. And it was no good. This

---

* Richi's boss, who to Pat's anxious inquiries always answered Richi was 'fine'.

† One probation officer.

man didn't have much contact with him. It was an unlucky choice. Richi resented his manner.

'Then, while he was on probation, he'd got Borstal. The probation officer said he didn't think he was a boy to be on probation. I can't remember what it was for. It was some time when the light was cut off. We only had candles, and nowhere to cook because we had an electric stove. And I was very depressed, not doing much but lying in bed. There didn't seem no point in getting up. I can't remember what it was for, but it was some silly little thing. I know. I was in bed, and he come in, and said could he have five shillings to go up the caff and have a meal, because he hadn't anything to eat all day. It was about twelve o'clock at night.

'I begged him not to go out. I dunno why. I just didn't want him to go out again. You know, he seemed ever so confident . . . slap-happy. He said "Don't be silly. You worry too much. I won't be five minutes."

'Next thing I know, it's morning, and somebody's crashing on my bedroom door. I live at the top of the house. And there's two plain-clothes men there. So they said they'd got him up Upper Street, and I could go up. They went in his bedroom. I asked them if they had a search warrant, and they said no, but they could get one. And I didn't bother. I thought there's nothing there, only his bed. So I didn't bother any more, just let them go in.

'So from there he went to Old Street, and then to the Sessions, and he got a Borstal. He'd got through this caff round the corner, through the ice-cream window, and gone upstairs. And when they saw him he was just sat in an armchair. The man said he hadn't attempted to take anything – just sat in a chair. I dunno, maybe he was taking pills or something.

'I spoke for him, but he still got a Borstal. And he went to a Borstal just past Henley-on-Thames. He seemed to get on all right there. He took up boxing again. He liked the boxing instructor. And while he was there, he did a course in painting and decorating. I was thrilled about this, because I thought if he likes that he can use his own imagination, he can use colours. I thought, he's done it because he's really interested in this kind of work. But as it happened, he was doing it because it was the best of the three that was offered; he didn't really like it.

'And while he was in there, a girl came to the house, a very nice girl. And she said she'd known Richi since they were kids – they used to go swimming together – and could she have the address of the Borstal because she'd like to write to him. And she used to write a card or a letter every day. And her mother and father had known him a lot, as it transpired. So she came on the visit with me.

'But before this, I was expecting Susan. Richi didn't know anything about it. So I didn't tell anybody at all – not even Nancie.

'I stayed indoors as much as I could. I didn't show, fortunately, very much, as she was a small baby. I was up the wall with worry. Nancie didn't know till I was eight months, nor did the doctor.

'So I thought, this'll just knock Richi for six. I thought, I'll have the baby adopted, and he won't know.

'When I was in hospital, I was very disturbed, crying and that all the time. Nancie came to the hospital, and kept saying "Let me write to him." And I just didn't know what to do.

'In the end, a family friend, Brian Robbins – his wife and him lived opposite – and I used to go to him. He was a writer and did those mobile things – The lady came about the adoption, and filled in forms. I didn't see the baby in the hospital, because I was afraid if I did I couldn't give her away. Brian had met Nancie by then, and he phoned her, and said, "Somebody's got to do something! I'm going down to the Borstal, and I'm going to tell him."

The Train Back

'He came down to the hospital to tell me what he'd done, the same time as Richi's letter arrived. And she gave me the letter from Richi, and she was going to say I had a visitor, when I knew Richi didn't know I was in the maternity hospital, and when I saw his letter I was screaming because I thought someone'd told him. Which, of course, he had.

'The sister, she was lovely. She was a coloured sister. And she opened the letter. She was saying "Read it! Read the letter! Read the letter!"'

'So I started to read it. He said, "Dear Mum, Brian's been down and told me about the baby. How dare you think of giving away my baby sister. You've never even wanted to give me away, and I've been nothing but a bloody nuisance. And anyway, I always wanted a baby sister. So you stop crying and get well. I bet she's a little smasher. And I'm looking forward to taking her swimming when she's a bit older. Love – Richi."'

This was the first time Pat broke down in front of me.

She wiped the back of her hand across her face, and went on.

'He came home from Borstal, and he eventually got a good job, with some gas company. He used to go to these things that were blowing up.

'And he had Ann then. He's never had any girl but her.

'Then things began to go a bit wrong between them. I suppose after being in Borstal he didn't want to feel tied down. He wanted to be free. And finally she was seeing someone else at the same time as seeing him.

'But they never made a clean break, because her parents were fond of him, and encouraged him to come to the house just the same. And they were on friendly terms.

'Then she got engaged secretly to this boy. Unfortunately her mother never thought she would. I think she was misled by her own desire for Ann to end up with Richi. She'd told Richi, "Don't worry. I know where her heart is."

'Richi was on night-work. I'd moved to Hackney, by then. And about four o'clock in the afternoon, he said he'd go over to Islington, because his mate's girl was twenty-one, and as he couldn't go to the party he wanted to take her a little present he'd bought her.

'But unfortunately, he called in to Ann's mother's house first. And she was looking a bit down, a bit depressed. And he asked her what was the matter. And he felt it was something to do with him. And he insisted on her telling. And although Ann had asked her mother not to say anything to Richi as she wanted to tell him herself . . . anyway she told Richi that they were unofficially engaged, that David had bought the engagement ring that day.

'He was very upset. He went in the pub and got drunk. He went round to her cousin, and asked him to drive him back home to my flat. And that's the first time I've seen Richi cry. And he said, "Mum, why has she done this to me? She knows I'm doing everything to show her how much I love her." He'd never worked so hard. He was working all the hours God sent, because he was trying to save up to buy an engagement ring for her at Christmas.

'And on the night she had the official engagement party, I was away. And when I came back he told me that he'd shot the man. He'd never fired a shot in his life before, but it went right through the man's heart.

'He doesn't want to get off. He just wants to know how long. I think he's entitled to know how long. All he wants is a date. He hasn't got anyone in his corner. He just wants to know how long!'

It seemed a good place to break.

Chapter Nine

I love you, Harry.
And I love you, Susie.
I love you, Leila.
I love you too, Susie.
I love you, Harry.
I love you too.

Later Pat took up the thread again. Pat was confused for a few sentences; and certainly this man she started to describe seemed an intruder, someone who had drifted by mistake into a three-fold love affair and drifted out again. She soon picked up the clear line once more.

'. . . At that time I was living with a man. I'd talked it over with Nancie. He had a good job, painting and decorating. And I liked him and that. That's where I was that Christmas, up in Preston with his family. They'd asked me to come up with Susan.

'But up there he was different. Like he came in drunk, and I thought well it's Christmas; but his mother started talking, and I thought "It looks as if she's had this worry with him all the time." Next day he went out and stayed out. And his mother said "You shouldn't let him out on his own." And I thought "She thinks we're married." When he come in at night, he was bleeding. He'd been in a fight.

'Then on television, I saw the news. And I thought "That's where Richi goes." And I knew he was depressed about Ann. And I wanted to get back!

'When we got back, Richi opened the door. I'd already had a row with this man, told him not to come. But he

insisted on coming back. Richi looked at him and said
"What's he been doing?" I said "I dunno. He's been in a
fight. He's been drunk."

'Richi got in a state, and said "What am I going to do? I
might have to go away for a long time. I don't want to leave
you with someone like this." It all come out in a rush – from
both of us. So he said "Come in here! I've got to talk to you!"
And he pulled my head down on his lap, and he said "What's
going to happen to you if I go away?" So I said "What do you
mean – go away?" He said "I think I've shot a geezer. I
think he's dead." He said "I'm scared, Mum. It's a topping
job."

'I didn't believe him. I thought he'd been taking pills or
something. I said "You probably imagined it." All the next
day I didn't believe him. And then . . . I wasn't sure . . . Oh,
I don't know . . . Then the following day Richi went back to
Islington. So I began to think he *must* have imagined it,
because I didn't see nothing about it.

'Then, when he was out, the police come. They just pushed
me out of the way. They said "You know who we are" – and
they were in! They just went everywhere. They said they
were looking for the gun. But I mean, I didn't even think
to look for a gun because I didn't think he'd done it. It
didn't make sense to me.

'They took Richi in for questioning. They took in all the
boys who were there on that night, then let them all go.
But two nights after, they came over to the flat where I was
living in Hackney, about eight of them or more, in plain
clothes. Richi wasn't in. He'd gone over to Islington.

'But on his way back to my block, they must have been all
round the flat. And someone rang a bell. And I knew by the
way everyone rushed out that it was a signal, so I rushed out,
because I thought if he struggled they might hurt him!

'They had his arms like that.* He said "Take a good look

* Pinned back.

at me. There's not a mark on me now. So you'll know if you see anything later that they've done it."

'I ran out and stopped a car, and asked if he was going to Islington to take me to Geoffrey.* I wanted someone to go straight to the police station, because I thought if there was someone in it from the outside they'd know, and they wouldn't give him a beating-up or something.

'At that Christmas, there were quite a few murders. A boy who stabbed someone, he was in with Richi; his mother used to come back with me, and she used to say her boy was always talking about Richi; he said if it hadn't been for Richi, he'd have killed himself. They had to give Richi tablets. They all cry at night, you know, and they said if Richi would only give way he'd be better, but he doesn't like to cry in front of the others, to upset them. All the warders say, "If he sees someone down, he always . . . you know." There was one boy there, never got a visit, nothing. And Richi said to me "Could you bring two dinners on one plate so's I can give him something? He's got a mother and father but they don't even drop him a line." And that's how he was – always caring about other people (no angel, mind you). I suppose that's why I liked him. Well . . . I loved him.

'When he was in Brixton I don't know if they specially pick the men for that wing – I was told they did – they were really decent men; they'd always amuse the baby so you could have a little talk . . . She was young, it was a long way and she was tired and she would cry and Richi would get upset; they would always come back to the gate with me and Bess,† and say "He's a real man. He's always trying to cheer the others up. He'll be all right," they said. "He knows he's got to do time and he'll accept it. If he gets a square deal, he'll be all right." Out of all the warders I've met in different

* Geoffrey Rankin of the Family Service Unit, Islington.
† Ann's mother.

places, and out of all the police, they were really the most understanding in that visiting room.

'I didn't go the first time to the court, 'cos Richi said it was too far, and with the baby . . . and it was bitter weather. And it was only formal. But the other times I was at the court all the time, and so was Ann's mother; she come with me.

'In the magistrates' court, the boy said he stole the gun from the place where he worked – he was the boy in the crowd of them having a drink together. He had it in his pocket that Boxing Night, in this pub. And he said to Richi, "Will you mind this gun and get rid of it for me?" And Richi said yes, he would, and took it. Then they had a last drink at this Camden Head pub, the next pub, and they were too late – the man said the bar was closed; and Richi was stood in there with one boy, and the others were all standing outside laughing. But the pub was full of coloured people because there'd been a christening or something. And one of the boys that was with Richi run in and said a coloured man was hitting a young boy. And Richi ran out, and he fired the gun, as far as I know.

'In the court, the boy that gave him the gun said he wasn't even sure himself that there was a bullet in it. They said "Did you tell Chapman there might be a bullet in it?" and he said "No sir." And Don said to me the other day "He couldn't have meant to shoot anyone. Because I was in the line of fire. If I hadn't happened to duck he would have shot me, and we're the best of mates."

'But I don't think Richi really remembers anything. I think he feels he's really responsible – that the bullet went in the man and that's all he knows. Because Don says they were just laughing about and joking, and they don't even know who went in to the pub to Richi and said "Somebody's getting hurt" . . . there was too many of them. And the boy in the court, the boy . . . I don't know if he was telling the truth – he said "I was talking to Richi, but I was looking the other way while I was talking, and all I heard was a bang behind me." I said to Richi, "One of your mates must know." But he said, "Look, it won't help to take anyone else with me. The man's dead, and that's that."

'But on the day of the trial, I don't know anything. Only what people told me after. Because they didn't even let me stay in the court room. They got me out of there by a trick.

'And his mate's mother went, Mrs Loval, Eddie Loval's wife, and the two boys. And she says the first thing Richi did in the court was look around for me. And he caught sight of her, and spreads his arms out like bewildered, and he kind of mouthed it – "Where's my Mum?" And she didn't know – she couldn't think what had happened. Even Bess didn't know, and I'd gone to the court with Bess and Nancie in a taxi. Bess wanted to speak on Richi's behalf; they told her she had to come out of the court as she was a witness for the defence, and when she saw me going into the room she had a feeling something was going wrong and she got hold of the solicitor and said "What's happening?" And she said "You will call me when it's my turn to speak?" And he said "None of the witnesses are being called." Everyone wanted to speak for him but he said "None of them." He said to her "I wouldn't bother to go back into court. It'll all be over in a few minutes." So she said "I don't care if it's one second. You can't keep me out, and I'm going back," she said. "That boy needs somebody in his corner." But I didn't know nothing, I was like a prisoner in a bloody room.'

She started to tell me again.

'I was bracing myself to go through with the trial no matter how long it lasted. I didn't say to anyone I couldn't face it or I couldn't stand it. The solicitor said "There's been some little hitch, some delay; perhaps you'd like to wait in here." That was some little room, with a matron in hospital uniform. By this time, I was getting distressed, because I was afraid once they started they wouldn't let us back, and I kept saying to Nancie, "Let's get back to the court"; and she didn't understand – she naturally thought we *were* going back. And then the Matron was saying "I'll get you a nice cup of tea. You'll be better in here." And then I understood – I wasn't going back in the court room!

'And I thought, surely no one can legally do this? I hadn't been making any bother. I'd just been sitting quiet, waiting for everything to start, and waiting for Richi to be brought in. If Nancie hadn't been there, I'd have forced my way at least out of that room, even if they could have stopped me getting into the court itself. But I didn't know what to do by then. I was in such a state – I didn't know what to do. I was crying. *I* felt like a prisoner, and I was only his mother.

'I cursed myself that I was so bloody stupid to let them push me around. You think they must know. You think they're your friends. Mrs Loval said Richi looked at the judge and said "I don't know what it's all about." He must have been so worried at not seeing me in court, he must have thought "They're right. She's in the mental home already." Because he knew damn well if I broke both legs I'd be there.

'Who is it who decides your mother's not well enough to take it? Who is it decides your mother can't stand by you, that she isn't strong enough to go through with it? I said to him, "Richi, why did you believe them! Why did you let them railroad you like this?" He said "They said you wasn't well enough to come." He said to me, "If nothing is done, I'll top myself, or I'll get out." Not to know when you're coming out . . . to be terrified to put a foot wrong . . . especially a boy who they're saying is subnormal . . . A million people went to speak for him, but weren't called.

'They said, "You know your mother can't stand a five days' trial. Plead guilty with diminished responsibility."

Diminished responsibility! My Richi can't use words like that. He doesn't know what words like that mean.

'They had no right! I was expecting a long trial. I was expecting the trial to go on five days. Nancie had even made arrangements for the baby to go into a nursery. Course I wanted a long trial. Things that could have helped him never came out in the magistrates' court. Everyone was going to speak for him at the Old Bailey.

'They took me and Nan into an office . . . a matron was there . . . I thought Richi must have committed suicide. This matron was fussing around me saying "Have a cup of tea. Lie down." All I wanted to do was to get back into court. They were driving me mad.

'And then Nancie said – she was getting angry by this time – she said "I won't have you distressed like this; it's stupid!" She said "I promise you, after the court breaks for lunch and it starts again we'll go back." And just as she said that, his mate* burst into the room, and the barrister was running after him and his wig was all sideways, and Bob just threw his arms out wide, and said "They've done 'im! They've done 'im!" And I was screaming "You bastard!" to the barrister. And he was saying "I wanted to tell her myself! I wanted to tell her myself! You had no right to burst in." And Bob said "You wanted to tell her yourself? You're bent. You've done nothing!" he said. And I was screaming because all the time they'd kept me in the room I was afraid someone was going to come in and say he'd hung himself or something, because I couldn't see any other point in keeping us in there. And I'm still frightened that'll happen, with a sentence like this!

' . . . And I was laying down on a couch – they made me lay down – and he† was squatted down on his heels and he was saying "You must believe me. We did it this way

* Richi's mate, Bob.
† The barrister.

because this way he's got a chance of coming out in four to five years."

'I tried to tell him Richi wasn't even hoping to come out in four to five years – he was *expecting* to get ten years, he told me that when he was on remand. They didn't do him any favour because now he doesn't know whether he's doing ruddy five, ten, fifteen, nothing.

'The Assistant-Governor tells me he mustn't be allowed to believe such a thing, that no one with that kind of sentence ever gets out within the time.

'The barrister told me this life sentence would only be four or five years. But the Assistant-Governor said this was nonsense . . . He said "A little while ago we were very concerned with Richi's mental health, due to the type of sentence. But he seems a bit calmer now."

'That's why it's such a strain visiting. He keeps asking me what I'm doing. He kept saying "I don't want them to open the gates and let me out. I just want to know how long." He says to me "You can't do your bird this way."

'And you see he's only a young boy. He looks to older men to advise him. And they tell him the same thing – he won't get out. At first I used to tell him not to listen to them. I said to him, "Look – the barrister knelt down by the side of me – he must know what he was talking about." But when the Assistant-Governor tells you that the boy's right, he won't get out in four, five years, that he'll do a life sentence, well what's the point of them reducing it to manslaughter in order to give him a chance! 'Cos that's what the judge said to him. I can't go on visiting Richi and reassuring him, "Don't worry. You'll get out," when the Assistant-Governor tells me I mustn't say that to him.

'. . . Then after – you know, you can wait about an hour and see them after the sentence – he was just trying to cheer me up. But through glass I couldn't explain that I was forcibly kept out of there. It wasn't till the sentence – "inde-terminate" you know – began to prey on his mind . . . some months after, on a visit at the Scrubs, we were both getting agitated, I said to him "You did nothing! Surely you could have done something to save yourself! I couldn't help you – they shut me up and I didn't know what was going on!" And he said "Don't shout at me. I did it for your sake."

'I was flabbergasted. I said "What do you mean?" And he said "They said to me 'Your mother can't stand the strain of a long trial.' They said 'Plead guilty, son.'" And he did.'

RICHI

Chapter Ten

It was quite true, what Pat had said – that she was shut up by a trick, kept out of court, while Richi was told to plead guilty on grounds of diminished responsibility. I half thought at first that it was ignorance of procedure on Pat's part, or awe at our mighty institutions, and then I half thought it was environmental paranoia. But when I went to see Richi's solicitors I had many talks and I read many documents. I found she was factually and entirely right.

And as a result, I uncovered a situation that was as fantastic and ironical as only a situation that is played blind can be.

Pat's tender relationship with Richi and his with her was coloured by a desperate attempt to preserve some sweet fantasy of how life should be. The lawyers too had a fantasy, but there was no desperation in it. It was one they had chosen to play because they enjoyed it – and it was the same rose-coloured fantasy, in which indeed we are thinking not of the other person but of our dream of ourselves. When this fantasy is played by people with power it becomes alarming. And I began to wonder how much of our society is built on this fantasy, and destroyed by it.

I stood by the heavy files of the Islington Gazette and turned the pages backward. Back through the everyday happenings of the neighbourhood to Christmas 1965, when Richi killed a man.

June, 1966
Nineteen-year-old Irishman stabbed woman he loved – jealousy.

'Robbery with violence'.

Numerous charges of 'living on immoral earnings'.

Man shot. (An axe featured in this case . . . also in another; it seemed to be a local weapon, perhaps because it was kept for chopping wood?)

NSPCC case – man and baby son.

Cafe knifing.

May

Murder of licence manageress.

Man's indecent behaviour with seven-year-old girls.

Two claims of frame-ups by police.

Trying to bash mate's head in with brick.

Knifing policeman.

Robbery with violence.

Man claims was kicked at police station.

Forty-eight teenagers in street row, armed with bottles.

Rape.

Protest campaign by people living in tenement block known locally as 'The Crumbles'.

April

Two teenagers in knife fight.

Police Inspector accused of assault at police station.

Youths found guilty of possessing offensive weapons – various knives and a spanner.

Three women beat up another woman.

Rape.

Rape.

Richard Chapman (it says 'age 20'). Charged at Old Bailey with 'purposeless and motiveless killing', of Eric Joel Yethman, St Ann's Road, Tottenham.

Prosecuting Counsel says he was handed pistol at previous Pub (Crown and Anchor) by friend who asked him to get rid of it; the shooting happened at the 'Camden'. He saw one of the coloured men go for one of the little boys.

Rough-handling by police.

Rape.

A seventeen-year-old, known locally as 'The Killer', convicted of – among other things – wounding a fourteen-year-old boy, shooting at a policeman, robbery with violence, and sentenced to five years. Six of his friends appeared with him, charged with conspiracy to silence witnesses, and with various charges involving carrying weapons.

Armed robbery.

Grievous bodily harm (with a dart).

'Wild West' shoot-out in pub.

Petrol-pump attendant threatened with iron bar.

March

Milner Holland Co., set up in 1963 to examine London's housing black spots, said:

Islington has largest number of overcrowded houses – 9,080.

Islington has largest number of houses in multiple occupation – 59% and increasing.

Islington has largest number of houses without bath, hot and cold water, or wc (77%), and that only Canonbury, which aims at relatively well-to-do buyers, was relatively decent. Sir Milner gave examples of living in Islington: landlord threatening to cut throat of tenant, or poison her, unless she paid the old rent instead of the one fixed by the tribunal; landlord putting rats in room; landlord saying 'Quit or be killed'.

Indecent assault.

P.C. drunk and unfit for duty.

Chasing youths with a brick.

The Train Back

February

Hitting man on head with a hammer – fined £25.

Living on immoral earnings.

13 February. Richard Chapman sent for trial from Old Street last week to Old Bailey.

Indecent assault.

A man, his four sons and two other men, accused of mailbag robbery.

Numerous shoplifting offences of tiny amounts (e.g. a jar of Bovril and a piece of soap) or of stealing food (1 lb. of butter, or milk), often saying it was for the children.

Living on immoral earnings.

Living on immoral earnings.

Shooting in a pub by a nineteen-year-old who borrowed the gun from his girlfriend to frighten a man who had 'made his life hell'.

Man stabbed in street after pub-crawl.

Man jabbed bottle into another man's face, after waiting for him for 3 weeks – said the first man had attacked him 7 months before.

Youth attacks boys' club.

Several places gutted by fire.

Very many drugs cases.

January

Unemployed man refused money by NAB returned, put his six-month-old baby on counter, and said 'All right, you feed him.'

Five accused of Christmas Day shooting (seventeen to nineteens), with intent to murder, inside and outside pub.

Malicious shooting.

Stealing milk.

Richard Chapman at Old Street Court.

Woman shot on bus.

Richi

Father assaulted nine-month-old son.

Girl steals milk – twenty brothers and sisters.

Firm specializing in tape recorders and transistors had its fifth break-in since Christmas Day.

Five men appeared on remand charged with shooting barman.

Youth stole three guns – one later sold to someone else and 'used in serious crime'.

Police Inspector accused of planting weapon on youth.

Indecent assault on small girl.

Battle in Chinese cafe.

Another home gutted.

December

Phone boxes rifled.

Father accused of assaulting four-year-old son.

Boy stabbed another after dance.

Richard Chapman case.

John McEllingot ('The Killer') case.

School caretaker accused of offences against girl.

Living on immoral earnings.

These all happened over Christmas holiday:

Man smashed glass into friend's face in pub so that he needed seventy-six stitches, because he'd put a drinking straw in his glass.

Stole to give sister a present.

Stole to give mother a present.

Another eighteen-year-old youth charged with murder on Christmas Day.

Electrician playing darts shot down in pub.

Barman shot from car as he left pub.

Jamaican shot and died instantly as he left pub – Richard Chapman case.

Teacher shot from moving car outside pub.

The Train Back

Policeman shot at house.

Twelve youths charged with fighting together on Christmas Day.

Police swoop on cafes – Scotland Yard campaign begins, to clear up violence in Islington.

The police, the psychiatrists, everyone, said the killing was motiveless. As for me, I wondered whether, in a district where violence was commonplace, with all his personal terror unacknowledged and anger at people he loved thrust resolutely out of sight – and such a need to keep love – I wondered whether it was surprising that Richi, drunk and perhaps half-drugged,* should have fired a gun that was in his pocket by chance, slipped in his hand by an acquaintance who asked him to get rid of it for him – and that he should have fired at a complete stranger – a *stranger* who he thought was hurting a young boy? I said to myself, sometimes people get in the way of a shout of despair, and, poor devils, are killed by it.

* Richi, like many of the local boys, took drinamyl (purple hearts).

Chapter Eleven

783 R. Chapman
Dear Bernice,

I would like to thank you for your letter. Also for the help wich you are giving me. I think it only right that as you are trying to help me, that it is only fair for me to see you and to tell you everything that happend, I don't know why, but I would like to feel that you belive me.

I dont expect for one minit that anybody should pat me on the back and send me home, Belive me I know more than anybody what it is like to know that you have caused a person's death, it is with me every minit of every day.

What is the truth is that this was completely unintentional in fact an accident, to be honest I dont realy no how it happend its still very hard to belive, All I do no is I cant carry on much longer like I am.

Iv had some knocks in my life and always been able to face up to them but Im afraid things are going from bad to v·orse the worry is driving me of my head, if things go on much longer like they are Ill end up in Broadmore.

Im sorry if this sounds full of self pity. Belive me pity is a thing Iv not got much use for, Its help Im asking for, If you see a copy of the Judge's remarks to me.

You will see that he said he wanted to explain the reason for the sentence wich he gave me. He then went on to say, the more I show him what Im worth the les my time will be. I would have thought that the place to show my worth is out-side, In here you have got to behave yourself. There is no choice.

Some of the fellows study in here perhaps thats what he ment.

This Iv tryied to do, but it just isn't any use. I read a book and cant keep my mind on it for very long.

Yet I no of people who have got five or seven year sentences for manslaughter, Wer the Judge has called them all soughts of thug's and animals, in fact were he thought there was nothing good to show him.

79

Yet these people have a date with which they can look, plan, and work for, its a hope for them.

for all I know I could get out tomorrow, next week, or a hundred year's time, I somtimes feel that it would have been better if the judge had called me all the thug's and animals there is perhaps I would have got the same chance as these people.

Well Bernice if you should ever like to see me, Ill be glad of the chance.

There is one thing I would rather you didn't show this letter to mum, as Iv tried my best not to let her know how I feel, as she has had more than her shair of worry. This was one of the thing's used to persuade me to plead guilty to manslaughter.

Which I feel, and other's have told me was bad advice, In a case as seriouse as mine, I think the court should have herd everything rather than the bare facts. there was many people who wanted to speak for me who did not get the chance and I feel I should have spoken myself at least they could have decided what kind of person I am much better.

As it was the corts exsepted the lesser charge, so they must have Exsepted my case in part, So the charge would have been reduced any way, As the law dosent do favour's on deals, So they must be right in thinking this, even the police in my case said they didnt think there was any intent or that there was any color predudis involved. Inspector Forbes in charge of the case told my mother if there was any help he could give to get in touch with him. Im sure this offer of help would not have been given if he thought me some kind of thug killer.

As Iv said before I dont expect a pat on the back. Iv done things I shouldn't have and expect to pay for them, Im just asking for a chance to prove myself, If I didn't feel I deserved this chance I would not ask for it.

Well Bernice I will close now, There is one thing, do you think it better if I saw you without Mum as I don't like talking about it in front of her, it only upsets her and makes me feel bad. Id like to thank you very sincerely for everything.

Yours faithfully,
Richi.

ps. I don't no wether to put Miss or Mrs so if Im wrong hope you understand.

Richi

Bernice comes into this, because someone who works in a prison sent for Pat and told her – unofficially – that he was appalled at what had happened and advised her to get in touch with *Justice*.* Pat had never heard of *Justice*. She asked Nancie, at the Family Service Unit; Nancie was just leaving for Sheffield, so fixed for her to talk to Bernice, another F.S.U. case-worker, who got in touch with *Justice* for her.

But *Justice* said the case wouldn't be reviewed for another two years, and that if Richi tried to get a definite date he would make matters worse for himself.

Hello Leila,
Thank you for your letter. Mum has told me about you and I am looking forward to meeting you. As far as how I feel towards Mum and little Sue go, well there is not really enough words to say, exsept I am proud to be able to say I'm part of the family. My luck was realy good when I got a mother and sister like Iv got.
I've put a v.o.† in with this letter for this coming Friday if that is alright with you, as if I no what day you are coming it gives me a chance to get my gear pressed.
I don't really no what else to say at the moment, and to be honest for me to fill one of these letters up is nigh on impossible. Looking forward to meeting you be lucky.

Richi.

The men in the Scrubs had been making a drink from metal polish and fruit juice, and one of them died and another went stone blind. The blinded one was the chap Richi had been taking his exercise with, a young chap. 'Depresses you when it happens to your mate,' Pat told me.

* *Justice* is the British section of the International Commission of Jurists; they are concerned with law reform.
† Visiting Order.

The Train Back

I sat in the waiting-room, waiting for Richi's name to be called, on a crowded railway-station bench with a railway-station lavatory behind me; but this was a prison. And I remember a woman came in, a little girl pulling at her skirt, a tiny baby in her arms.

'You'd better go now, before we go in, or you know what'll happen,' she said, meaning the lavatory . . . 'She can't manage on her own. Will you just hold him while I take her?' Then just as the middle-aged woman on the other bench obligingly held out her arms for the tiny baby, a warder came in and called out a string of names and we all went, the middle-aged woman, too, quickly giving the baby back. We all went. None of us dared give up a second of our visiting time. I looked back into the empty room – just the mother and baby there and a child too young to go alone, and the child was crying.

Sitting at the small table, Richi told me about the day of the trial.

'To start with, I didn't feel confident about the Q.C. They kept asking me about my life, my own life, and I don't like talking to people about that. Only once I saw the Q.C.* At least I think that's who he was. I had a lot of people said they wanted to speak for me. I gave the solicitor all their names and he said yes, they'd be called. Then the day of the trial this chap with a wig comes out and says they'll accept a plea of guilty for manslaughter, and that my mother was in a terrible state, and it would be the best thing for her. I said all right. I couldn't see what else to do. Myself, I thought it was more an accident than anything. What I didn't know was I couldn't go back on it. I never knew what was going on. First week I was here, the police officer said

---

* Richi's solicitor told me later that Richi in fact saw his Q.C. at least twice before the court, and once at the court – he also saw the junior counsel several times at Old Street. He would have been very dazed and confused, the solicitor says.

Richi

"Gor blimey, you ought to appeal." Next thing I know he brought in forms to make an appeal. Well, you have to have legal help for that; I didn't have nothing. I filled it in. All that happened was I got a thing back saying I'd lost forty-two days remission and my appeal was turned down or something. It was my own fault.

'I should have told Mum I'd appealed. I didn't tell her because straight away she'd have thought something good would happen. That's why I never told her nothing that happened in court. She's very nervous, Mum; she'd just get hysterical. So I thought I'd better get it over with.

'Mum's got no money. And in this, it's just all important. If you've got some bread like, it's all right; if not, it's just too bad.

'Mum's had a lot of worry all her life. She's had the rough end of the stick. It does me up, when she comes to see me. I'm sick for about three days after. To tell you the truth I'd rather not have visits . . . and little Susan, you know, she says "When you come back on the train . . ."

'Mum's like me. People like us we believe in luck. If your luck's in, you're all right. If it isn't, you're not.

'I've seen chaps been in for four or five years and they love the place; they feel at home. The judge he said it might seem harsh to give me a life sentence. What did he mean? If it seemed harsh, then he must have known it *was* harsh. He said he was giving me a chance to prove myself. How can you prove yourself behind bars? When you're behind bars you have to do as you're told, that's all there is to it.

'If I was in here for something else, I wouldn't mind like. It's not a nice thing to be in for. There was a chap in here, his baby was crying, he whipped it to death; he got five years. Another chap, he battered his wife to death; they give him a conditional discharge; they said something about diminished responsibility . . . he got nothing. They said it was better for his family if he got nothing. I can't understand.

Even the police said, "in this case we feel there was no intent"; and they also said there was no question of colour prejudice.

'You have to see doctors, you know, they give you tests; and they said it was diminished responsibility. So they reduced it to manslaughter. At the time, to talk callous, if I'd been found guilty of murder I wouldn't have been hung; I'd have got life; well, they reduced it to manslaughter, and I still got life. When they said diminished responsibility, I didn't know what it meant till everyone laughed . . . The court even accepts that a baby's crying is "provocation", and they get a sentence – five or six years.

'I'm not a violent person. I had a firm of geezers looking for me threatening all sorts of things, saying they'd cut me up, leave bits of me all over London. I just got out of their way, to keep out of trouble. I even went off with Jim and Bess.* They took Mum too. Jeez, camping, camping! Sleeping on the ground! Mum loved it! She would! She's mad! She used to box with me. She's mad, you know. Used to put on a pair of boxing gloves and wait for me and box me up. She's a lunatic. She's like one of the boys. My Mum, she knows so many people, it's mad. People used to come in – they might be just out of Wandsworth – or the family of a duke. That's my Mum. She's got loads of friends. I'm glad for her. I know she isn't on her own.'

It was an open visit, and I thought I would have an hour, but in fact I had nearly two, and Richi talked all the time because I was a friend of Pat's.

After a long time – because I was a little afraid to say it – I asked, 'Do you remember your father at all?'

'Yes I do. I remember more than Mum knows. She thinks she's kept things from me. She's like me, like that. We both of us keep things shut up, keep them away from each other, you know. But I remember them breaking the door down and finding my Dad with his throat cut. And I remember my

* They are Ann's – his old girlfriend's – parents.

Richi

Dad chasing Mum round the table with me in her arms. And once, Mum doesn't know, but I phoned the hospital – I wanted to see him, and I phoned the hospital but I was only a kid and they asked me how old I was and when I told them they said I'd have to ask my Mum. I never told her. She thinks I don't know anything. I was old for my years when I was a kid. She doesn't realize.'

Chapter Twelve

The morning I set out to find out what had really happened on the day Pat claimed she had been kept out of court by a trick, I had no idea Richi had now been labelled 'a trouble-maker'. I was simply set on finding out whether Pat's description of his trial was fantasy.

The facts, according to Richi's solicitor whom I talked to, were these. In 1965, he said, any boy who like Richi was twenty when first tried and twenty-one when convicted, could be hanged for killing by shooting. His lawyers had three possible courses of action. They could say he didn't fire the shot. But Richi had already told the police he did (though no one, incidentally, has been able to tell me if he had actually been charged when he made this statement, nor if he had been cautioned* before he made it, nor if he made it in writing or only verbally). They could say it was an accident. But – irrespective of how many of his mates were in the way – he had aimed the gun. They could claim 'diminished responsibility'. To do this, they would need a psychiatric report.

Three eminent doctors examined Richi. Their reports – which were never revealed, except to the judge; they were never read out in court, never seen by the jury, by Pat, or by Richi – stated that Richi was 'tense' – 'increasingly resentful of being questioned' – 'in particular disliked talking about his childhood and his domestic affairs' – 'has a belief that interference was being made into his affairs' – 'had a suspicious, restless attitude' – and a 'belief that he is

---

* If when he was actually charged, he had not been cautioned – that is, warned that anything he said would be written down and could be produced as evidence – the police were acting illegally.

condemned before he is tried' and showed 'arrogant unnecessary rudeness to the police when questioned' – 'is
secretly worried he might go like his father' – 'is a tense, inarticulate, rather backward individual, verging on aggres-
siveness, evasive and suspicious particularly in regard to
mental illness' . . . 'resentful and aggressive when any of his
many feelings of inferiority about personality or home life
are touched upon' . . . and 'described his drinking and drug-
taking as normal'. One said that Pat was 'an emotionally
unstable woman of no intelligence', and another that she
'has always kept a clean and respectable home together',
and another that she 'has suffered depressive phases' and
'has had in-patient treatment'.

The doctors had at least seen Richi. (Though what the
average 'top' psychiatrist – speaking with a well-to-do
English accent or a continental one, using syntax that to a
working-class boy is stylish acrobatics, with an attitude to
life and to people that has nothing in common with his own
experiences and his own relationships – what the average
'top' psychiatrist would make of a boy like Richi, and Richi
of him, is a foregone conclusion. I once talked to a West
Indian girl who lived in the East End, whom a social worker
had sent to a psychiatrist. She told me 'He was crazy. He
never said a word to me. I told him the most personal
things and he just wrote them down in a damned little
book, never spoke a word to help me. Who does he think he
is, to treat me like dirt?' And she walked out, and never
went back. So much for psycho-analysts, whose well-to-do
patients have 'out-patient experience' not 'in-patient experience', who belong so firmly to middle-class experience
and middle-class values.)

To Richi these men were bound to be seen as narks,
copper's mates; they were out to get him. (And of course he
was right. They were for the defence; they were out to save
him from hanging. But they were also out to get him. This

wasn't fantasy.) And when they asked him questions about his Mum and Dad, trying to make out his Mum and Dad were nutters and that he was a nutter too (and they *were* trying to make out they were nutters – this wasn't fantasy), of course he closed up; he got edgy. He was a working-class boy, and never having read Freud, or indeed anything very much, he tried desperately to protect his family from people who were clearly alien, and out to frame them. So they wrote him down as 'resentful . . . aggressive . . . suspicious . . .' (and they did this for his own sake – or rather, they did this to put over 'diminished responsibility' which would save him from hanging).

But Pat, who was written down as 'of no intelligence'? Not one of them had ever seen Pat. I didn't discover this till much later, at the end of the story. I had assumed they had interviewed her. But quite by chance I asked her what the psychiatrists had said to her all that long time ago, and she told me 'They never saw me. Nobody ever interviewed me. Nobody at all. *After* the trial, after the barrister had spoken to me, the solicitor tried to see me several times, but I refused – I had nothing to say to him – it was done. But eventually one day I did see him, and we had a short interview, in which I said nothing; I was still in a state of shock; and anyway I couldn't talk; I didn't know how to; I could only write, and nobody ever asked me to do that. Eminent! How could they call them eminent, when they didn't know they had to find the real boy! They didn't meet Richi. They met someone who was trying not to show any emotion, someone who was covering up.' She didn't know how startled I was. She thought I was asking what opinion they were framing of Richi, and I couldn't tell her I had been thinking about what opinion they had framed of her.

So I tried to find out tentatively whether she had behaved, 'unintelligently', during the weeks when Richi was remanded in Brixton Prison before the trial, and she said,

'Visiting him in Brixton every day, cooking him a meal daily and taking it, washing, ironing, and taking him clean laundry, looking after the baby and taking her too nearly every day, on three buses from Hackney Wick . . .'

And then she said, 'He can't bear pain or grief in his friends, Richi. And I'm the same. My only thought was, if I forced my way in would he see his mother forcibly evicted, and would they take his grief and anger as a sign of violence? I didn't know what to do. I couldn't do anything but cry. I was crying for help . . .'

So I got this bizarre picture of six legal men, determined to do their professional best for Richi, pacing up and down the corridors of the Old Bailey, discussing, arguing, going over and over the erudite possibilities. These were first-class trained legal minds, working conscientiously on a legal aid certificate, briefed by a humane, liberal-minded and hard-working solicitor and with a most unusual amount of sympathetic documentation. And what they decided was that they would keep the reports on Richi and Pat *from* Richi and Pat (which meant that they would not be read out at the trial, that Richi could never answer them, nor even know on what statements he had been sentenced), and that they would get Richi to plead guilty (with no explanation or warning to his friends and neighbours who had taken time off from work to appear as witnesses for him, and to support him) and that they would get his mother out of court by a trick, and keep her out of court by a trick (which would silence her). All this they did, genuinely, for the sake of Richi and his mother, neither of whom, they believed, would be able to stand hearing 'the truth' about their situation – or what the lawyers thought was the truth – or what the lawyers and psychiatrists decided it was politic to call the truth – without going round the bend. They did this with the best of intentions, which perhaps sometimes, when one is rather remote from one's beneficiary, can be a little presumptuous.

Maybe it's unbalanced to call it 'presumption' when what they did so efficiently achieved their main purpose which was to save Richi from being hanged?

Yet I discovered later, from 1964 no one was in fact hanged for murder because Sidney Silverman's bill abolishing capital punishment was already pending, and therefore hanging had already stopped. So Richi had been made to plead guilty, for what?

Well, at least one of them wonders now whether the decision they reached, pacing those corridors, was the right one. But he tells me he always does. Possibly, being the least powerful, he is the only one among that well-intentioned crowd who does not bustle on when 'the operation is successful' but stays to think of the patient.

Chapter Thirteen

Richi didn't tell Pat, or me, he was in chokey.*

I had been to see Ann, Richi's old girlfriend, and Bess, her mother; and they had filled in for me even more strongly the picture of Richi and Richi's situation.

Ann's baby was in a pram outside the window, a lovely baby, but Ann was bored with it, and bored with her husband and he with her – they had already separated – and bored with marriage; she was only nineteen. She must at any rate have thought David had more dash than Richi, who had never slept with her.

They told me about Richi, talking alternately, Bess starting.

'He was four months on remand, in Brixton. Pat and I went up every day.'

'I went too. One minute he thought it would be all right. One minute he thought it would go all wrong.'

'Pat used to be pretty upset. But she always put on a brave face for Rich.'

'Rich knew Pat was covering up for him. He always knew.'

'All those three months, Pat was in a terrible state, crying. There were times when she just used to clamp up, just sit there. We took her away a couple of times. Gradually she came round. She would have gone through the trial all right . . .'

When Ann went out to see to the baby, Bess confided to me, 'When Ann got engaged I think the bottom dropped out of everything. She's known him since she was eight. When he wanted to go out with her, years later when she was fourteen, he was man enough to come to us. This was his family.' (She meant 'We were his family.')

* Solitary confinement

'When Ann got engaged, he couldn't come any more. We couldn't even ask him to the party – we thought it wasn't wise. He wanted someone to hang on to – a family.

'If you done him a kindness, he never seemed to forget it. If he took our Ann out and kept her out late, he always came down next morning and apologized.

'He wouldn't let a fly hurt Ann. He put her on a pedestal.

'We don't tell him nothing.* We don't want to upset him. It's not fair.

'He knew Ann had this other boyfriend. He used to keep coming on the pretence of seeing us but I think really he wanted to see Ann. He just doted on her. I think he blew his top that night.

'I kept telling him Ann was only a kid; he'd find plenty of other girls. But you just couldn't shake him. I used to tell him she's spoilt; but he'd say "You don't understand her, she's all right." He never had anything but good to say for David. He said "He'll be good for Ann . . ."'

The same picture of Pat and Richi tenderly looking after each other, covering up for each other – the chink the law found when they said in their fatherly way 'Plead guilty, son,' adding 'it will save your mother distress'.† And the same picture of the boy who never hurt the people he loved and whose love he needed. Richi once said his girlfriend went out with another chap, and that if he were the kind of person to want to kill someone this is the man he would kill; but he had never attempted to hurt him. No, he never did. In the end he killed a stranger.‡

* She meant about Ann and David rowing.

† Richi's solicitor doubts that the police did say this last sentence. He thinks it more likely that it unconsciously arose from Richi's anxieties.

‡ From this point, the early draft of the book included letters that I sent to various appropriate people about Richi's case, and details of what happened. This began, however, to read like a day-to-day campaign for a date for Richi's release, rather than a book about Pat's life. This material has therefore been cut.

Chapter Fourteen

On Pat's kitchen table there is a wedding photograph, very gay and debonair. It shows a delightful girl, like a Vogue model, and a good-looking smiling boy, his hand spread in a Fred Astaire gesture – '*Made it!*' I asked Pat who it was, and she said 'It's Bob.' Bob I knew was Richi's mate.

So she started to tell me why he had flicked out his hand like that, impudently, wryly, triumphantly. The Islington gangs always want to be recognized, always want, Pat said 'to prove who was who'. And this particular gang, Jack just got on the raw because he would not recognize them at all; none of the three of them ever recognized a gang; they wanted a quiet life. Jack was Bob's brother.

So one night they sent a messenger round to Jack, to tell him to come out and fight. 'They want a meeting face to face, to prove something,' said Pat. Jack couldn't ignore it. He said to Richi and Bob 'What d'you think? Shall I take something?' 'No,' said Richi. 'You'll be a mug if you do. Bob and me'll keep a look-out. We'll see there's only him and you.' But Bob said, 'I dunno. You're my brother. You do what you think. We'll keep a look-out like Richi says.' At the last moment, Jack made up his own mind and took a knife.

Richi and Bob guarded the back alley. A woman sauntered by. They saw her turn her head, heard her scream 'Don't hit him with that axe! You'll kill him!' and then she ran down the street and they never found her again. They tried to, later, because they needed her, Pat said; but they never did. Jack stabbed the boy with his knife and the axe clattered to the ground.

By the time the police arrived, the axe had been

dismantled by the rest of the gang, Pat said, and become a wooden handle. Jack got two years.

Bob had always said that Jack would be best man at his wedding, so when he knew Jack was coming out he fixed the day. The night Jack came home, he and Bob went to the fish and chip shop, and standing in the long long queue, quietly, efficiently and with a minimum of fuss, Jack was stabbed. No one saw who did it, because no one knew for a long time that it had happened; the queue was tight, body pressed against body, and there was no blood. But everyone took it for granted it was one of the gang.

Bob got Jack to hospital, and another friend sat by his bed all night. In the morning, to everyone's surprise he was still alive, and looked like living. And Bob himself just made it to the registrar's office on time. And outside, showered with confetti, with a white lace bride – *Made it! No best man unfortunately but I made it!*

Weeks later, long after I thought I had finished this book, I went down to the Scrubs with Pat and Bess. The visits those two had! Pat laughing at Richi, flirting, coaxing him, cajoling him! I wanted just to sit there and watch the pair of them and marvel. But I couldn't.

The minutes ticked by in foolery. I took a deep breath, and spoke. (Pat knew what I was going to say. I had discussed it with her in the waiting-room.) 'Richi. We've got to get some good reports before the Home Office. Otherwise God knows when you'll get out. We *need* you to see the psychotherapists. If you don't, when your case comes up for review the Home Office won't have any reports to consider to help them decide about you. All they've got are reports saying you won't co-operate.' I went on talking. I could feel Richi was getting more and more tense, and I stumbled and swore to myself and went on talking, all the time thinking under the words,

'Let it be, let it be! They only have half an hour – let them have fun and games in it – let them laugh together a bit – let them be!'

When suddenly Richi turned on Pat. 'You think I don't remember anything! You keeping saying you'd kill yourself, I remember that! Saying you couldn't stand living this way any more – d'you think I don't remember! Do you know what it did to me! I keep remembering it! It scared hell out of me – it still does!'

Pat was shocked and white. He had never spoken to her like this before.

And then he turned to me. 'I'll tell you how it happened, that night. I've never told anyone. Remember I told you about a firm of geezers looking for me, drove me out of London? Well, when I came out of that pub, saw all that fighting, I thought they'd got me. I'd got that kid's gun in my pocket. I took it out and waved it, that's all. "Keep off!" That's all. I didn't even know it was loaded. "Keep off me! Don't come any nearer!" I must have squeezed it too hard, and it went off.'

We were all silent. Then Pat, very white now, said 'Why didn't you say? You could have said.'

'And have the gang after you and Susie!' said Richi savagely.

I had jotted down what Richi had said on my first visit with the screw edgily watching, and had never given it another thought. And the bits I had jotted down from the local paper when I looked up Richi's case – for instance, the boy called 'The Killer' sentenced (ironically) the same day as Richi, and the six or seven of his gang who were sentenced too, for conspiring to silence witnesses . . . and Bob's jaunty air in the photograph . . . I had never thought of putting them together.

Walking back to the station after the visit, very tired and rather dazed, I filled in the story.

After they'd tried to get Jack, who had finished up in gaol, they tried to get Bob and Richi. They drove Bob all over London. He always played it down when Pat was around. But one Saturday afternoon, when Susie was sleeping in her pram outside the flats, and Pat was upstairs and Richi was out, a whole mob poured down the street, waving broken milk bottles, yelling for Richi. Pat rushed out in her stockinged feet and snatched up Susie, gave her to her neighbour to keep safe, and rushed down the street half-crazy, pushing through the crowds who were screaming out that Richi was in a cafe somewhere, and they'd find him, drag him out, and kill him. People were leaning out of their windows, watching the horde as it streamed by like floodwater. Up the road the milkman was sprawled like a starfish against the side of his wrecked van. People said there were at least a hundred of them. They surged down the road. At the bottom, the betting-shop man rushed out and shouted 'I'm phoning for the police!' so they separated into two streams.

But they never found Richi. Pat didn't find him either. She came back exhausted, stockings cut to ribbons, her feet bleeding.

Later still, when the streets were quiet and deserted, Richi came back too. He gave her a grin, and said 'I hear someone's been looking for me.' And he added 'Cheer up, Mum. I'll make you a cup of tea. You look a bit shagged.'

But this time, she wasn't having it. She made him get out of London, made him get out by going with him. They all went, Pat, Bess, Susie, Jim, and Richi, pretending they were having a sudden holiday.

After that, she thought it had settled down – thought so because she hoped so. And when Richi fired a gun at a fighting crowd, she was as bewildered as anyone else.

When we left the Scrubs and got to the station, Pat and Bess sank into a seat while we waited for a train. Suddenly I realized that what was for me warm-hearted but intellectual exercise was for them a matter of life and death.

PAT

Chapter Fifteen

I had sent the first chapter of this book, very much shortened, to the *Guardian* and they were going to publish it. They asked me to take Tony Colbert, whom they wanted to illustrate it, to see the children. I took him to Pat's flat, and he photographed Susie playing with me, in the 'Princess Jasmine hat' – she calls it – that she puts on to 'phone' Richi in prison. And while this was going on Pat made tea and talked about a very brief seaside holiday they had had the previous week, a fiasco. Pat told it as a great joke – but I could hear the unspoken anger and outrage underneath. Later I said, 'Write this down the way you *truly* felt it. Write it for publication. But apart from that, keep writing about everything, everything you feel and think and remember, not with publication in mind, but to get it down and to send it to me. Just keep writing and writing. This is important.'

Later, after some prodding on my part because by then Pat was writing far more urgent things, Pat did actually write this incident down. The 'what a crazy bloody lark' tone had evaporated, and she wrote soberly, and with regard for the fact that it was for possible publication.

FIRST HOLIDAY

We were at the station bright and early. The case had been packed for days. Nothing was going to spoil our first holiday, mine and Susan's.

Susan and I talked about it night after night in bed together. I told her if I could find somewhere cheap, and if we didn't go mad, we could make it a whole fortnight.

The Train Back

The thought of two weeks at the seaside with Susan was almost too much to bear. The thought of it! I had spent a day with her at Brighton the October before and it had been one of the most memorable days of my life. We never moved from the beach the whole day. She never asked for anything, and we never stopped laughing, and I knew she loved the sea just as much as I did. The sound and smell of it, and the look of it. And I promised her going home in the train that we would go, and for two weeks if it was humanly possible.

So here we were at Victoria Station, before seven o'clock in the morning. Pevensey Bay, that was the place to head for. No need to book, friends said; the two of you should get fixed up easy. I had big ideas. A caravan, or chalet, I thought. Susan must be free to come and go – really free. I didn't want to have to say *sh!* not once.

We searched that place from end to end. I had to carry her most of the time. It was a very hot day, and already she seemed to be developing a chill. But we couldn't find anywhere to stay.

Then we saw a coach turn the corner. HASTINGS it said. And we climbed up into it, and I just slowly relaxed, and laid Susan on the seat beside me. She didn't stir, she was so exhausted. By the time we reached Hastings we had recovered our lost enthusiasm. Susan was ready to plunge in the sea and so was I – just to fall into those crashing foaming waves was all I could think of. So we went up to the top of the cliffs in the lift, and fell flat on our backs in the grass to think what to do.

Looking back, I realize that I was not very adult at the time, but it was gone four o'clock and it was important somehow that Susan should have something for herself from this day. She had been so patient, so uncomplaining, and at times it almost seemed that she was the Mum, saying things like 'Don't worry, dear' – 'Am I too heavy?' – and

'Cheer up, we'll find a nice lady who will let us stay.' But we didn't.

By now we were ready to go into anything. We went to every house with a little card in the window, but no one would give us a room. It was fantastic. Here was a seaside place, obviously gone to seed, with empty houses and hotels sticking out like sore thumbs on every corner almost, and yet turning us away, sometimes politely, and sometimes very rudely.

We had a great secret now, Susan and I. We had hidden the case in among some bracken on a steep incline off the cliff. 'Please God, it won't roll,' I thought. I could see the houses at the bottom, and I could almost imagine it crashing down into a little back garden. It held all our possessions, all Susan's clothes, all mine. But I had changed in the lavatory at the top of the cliff, and had on my swim-suit under my trousers and shirt. Oh that water. Never ever will seawater seem so cold, so luxurious.

We rode up and down the sands on a miniature railway for the sheer fun of it, and we were laughing out loud both of us, and people looked and they laughed. I thought 'Poor Sue. She's been under as big a strain as me.' And I realized that we should be trying once more to get digs somewhere, and that I was behaving like a child.

And suddenly the sun disappeared, it blew cold, and rain started to pour from the sky. The change affected me. I felt suddenly very unsure of myself, and very frightened, and it was as if everyone was aware of us and looking. And then I saw it – 'Double room to let. Bed and breakfast'.

I ran to the door. I was terrified someone might reach there before me. It was nearly ten o'clock. The sky had just opened, and the water dripped from us everywhere.

Yes. She had a room. She seemed very nice. I wanted to hug her. Wouldn't it be too expensive? Oh no, we had the money. Mentally I had readjusted my mind to spending one week by the sea. And then it came, that voice getting slightly more impersonal. Wouldn't I like to go somewhere cheaper?

I couldn't believe my ears. A child of four was standing there by my side, saturated with rain, it was dark, she had a room to let and I had the money to pay. I groped in my purse. I was silently begging her, '*Please!* My kid wants to stay here. She likes your seaside.'

But she was saying 'I don't really take in children.' 'You don't like children!' I was shouting – or at least it seemed as if I was; perhaps it was just the wind – '*Please*. Just for the night!' I pleaded.

'I'm sorry. I'd like to help you. But you see, I don't take in children.'

Poor dear little Susie. She was wonderful. That's why I love her. 'Let's go and get our case, and let's go home to London,' she said.

I wish you could have seen her, this tiny little four-year-old tackling those steps on the top of the cliff. At first I thought our case was gone. I was so tired, so sick of this seaside that had at first seemed exciting because of its link with history, that I almost felt glad. But then we found it. And I opened it up and fished about for dry clothes for Susie, and dragged out her raincoat.

Four people came running by. I let them go. I could have said 'Will you help me?' but I was too numb. And then they were all back round me, all talking at once. 'Here! Give me that! I'll take the baby! Give me that holdall!' Wonderful, wonderful people – two married couples, happy married couples, I'm sure they are. I won't ever forget them. No suspicion. No leading questions. Just seeing what a hell of a state I was in – running us to the station in their car, the wives saying 'The men will look after you, love.' Wonderful, wonderful people, who with these few kind words made the world seem a nice place once more.

I hope to God there will always be people like that for everybody.

On the evening of that day when Tony met Pat and me for the first time, and had heard Pat talk about 'that bloody lark at Hastings', he phoned me and said, 'I've been thinking about Pat. My mother lives at Littlehampton, and she'd love Pat and Susan to come and stay. They'd all take to each other at once and get on marvellously. I've just phoned her and checked it's all right. She says they should come as soon as they possibly can.'

This was the effect Pat had on people, on people open to her, people not in authority.

Chapter Sixteen

When she came back from Littlehampton, Tony sent both of us invitations to his exhibition of drawings of Vietnam. Many of them were children in hospital wards. Immediately after Pat and I had met there, Pat's writing started to flow into me, urgent writing. Sometimes three different pieces would arrive in the same post.

IRON COTS

Mum come and fetch her. I remember my sister shouting that out in the middle of the night. I thought, she means me. It had happened before. My mother used to put me to sleep in a big iron cot, and I remembered that cot very vividly today. All Tony Colbert's paintings were of children in big iron cots, and I felt very ill inside. I wanted to run but I wanted to curse and swear and plead for those kids – don't create more children like me. It just seems that even if they mend their limbs, who's going to mend their minds?

I don't know how to explain some things that happen. It's like this book, why I'm writing it. It's bloody hard. There's no one who can take Susan off my hands, and yet if I don't go on writing I think I'll explode.

I've got to start from the beginning. It seems I can't let myself off anything. And perhaps unconsciously that was what I was doing, trying not to admit that these things had happened and were happening again.

I was in a hospital. I didn't walk or talk. I just growled if people came too close, even nice people. I was strapped down somehow, because I remember how frightening, even terrifying, it was, and is even now, if the bedclothes are tucked in too tight – I wake up sweating with fear. I saw the doctor, and I was aware of what was being said between him and the sister. 'Why?' she said. 'Why?' Her hand was bleeding where I'd clawed her. 'I try to be as helpful as I can,' she said. And the doctor seemed sad as if he wanted more support, not angry, just sad.

I tried to speak. I don't know if I did say a word here and there, but I knew I could, and I had to tell him somehow. I tapped out a tune on his hand. At first I thought, he isn't listening; he must listen; I'll never speak again if he doesn't listen. And then he seemed suddenly to get the message. At first he just looked at the piano, and then he laughed and said 'She's a smart girl! She can't speak, but she can sing. And that's just what she's doing now. She's bloody well singing with her mind.' And that was the beginning of a long hard fight back, and if my memory can be trusted my first fight.

He had me carried to a piano in the ward each day, and he talked and played, talked and played, and the tears would first fall from my eyes and I cried out without a voice and with no movement of my limbs or my body, 'Don't give in!' It was as if I knew he was on to something and if for any reason he left the hospital I was lost for ever.

Gradually the tunes he played penetrated my brain, and I began to remember I had feet and legs, that I loved to dance, that I was having lessons before this happened – the lady was teaching me for free. He saw it! The slight movement, my toes tapping, my feet making dance steps. Before that at first only my mind was dancing – you know what I mean? – the message hadn't reached my feet. But I was remembering myself, who I was, and most important the last thing that happened before the black-out, and that was the dancing lessons.

He played tune after tune and it was as if I was communicating with a psychiatrist. Not that I knew anything about psychiatry then, but I was aware he was different, not just an ordinary doctor, and that somehow I had the answer somewhere in me, but that I needed him to help me find it. 'Let her bang on the keys,' he told the sister. But I saw red. I mean it! Big orange and red flashes. And I growled. It was all I could do, but I had to make him know, and I was desperate to speak the words, but I couldn't. My hair was wet, and I tried to make him look at me. And that's when it came to me, 'Tap out the notes on his hand.' And I did, over and over, and he took my fingers and pressed them down on to one note after the other, but in rhythm and with melody, and he laughed, and I laughed, because it was as if I was saying 'I'm not tone-deaf.' And perhaps that's what I'm trying to say now. Don't give up. Let's all try to communicate with people, or we might just as well stay at home and sleep in iron cots. Who knows, perhaps that would have been my lot if it hadn't been for that doctor – a lifetime in an iron cot somewhere or other. It's been rough, very rough, but at least it hasn't been a complete waste. I was eight years old at the time.*

Pat was zigzagging backwards and forwards. I could not say to her 'Write about this now. Write about that', because she was writing down what was happening to her again. She was feeling it again, living it through, and when she finished writing – and her writing seemed to be automatic – often she was crying. And when this 'trance', as she called it, came over her, she did not know what she was going to write, or find out. I have not arranged her writing so that it illuminates her past, neatly. I tried to, but it would not work. I would have had to rewrite it and telescope it, and I

* One thing I had asked Pat – to try always to fix her age.

did not want to alter one word of Pat's, nor blur the gradual knowledge of herself that she found, going back through a past she thought she did not know.

It's flying, Denny, it's flying! I was so excited. Denny was my friend, the boy next door. He sang in the choir. I went to hear him sing solo, but all the time I was thinking what lie to tell if it got back to my mother that I had gone to another church. Perhaps she wouldn't have been angry, but I knew I couldn't tell her, so I would lie if she did find out. We were thrilled with the kite. We'd made it between us – well, I don't think I'd done much; I'm not much good with my hands; I gave him good advice, perhaps. But we were up on the sand dunes and the kite was in full sail, and I felt the string tugging at my hand, and I wanted to lift my feet off the ground and sail off too. I could tell things like that to Denny, and even if he didn't understand he'd just grin, but not unkindly, and I could bear it. We stayed up there all afternoon, and then it was tea-time. But I didn't want to go home to tea, and Denny didn't seem easy about leaving me up there alone. So I went home with him. But suddenly the peace was over. Some bigger boys came tearing out of their back gate, and I suppose I expected them to know what the kite had done for me, the feeling of peace and joy I'd felt. I started to tell them. Maybe I used words they didn't understand. Maybe I looked different for a second, not so sullen, but they just laughed. They said 'Don't play with her, Denny. You know she's mad.' They made a grab for the kite. They broke it. Denny rushed at one of them, and I went to help him and suddenly they forgot Denny and the kite, and were all rushing at me, and I seemed to go berserk. I bit and kicked, and all the time they were saying I was mental and mad and using words like that, and I saw those red streaks again, and then my big sister was shouting 'Leave her alone!' And the boy's face was scratched and bleeding, and he was saying 'You want to get her locked up again?' And my sister took me home. But I couldn't understand why she was angry with me. I never seemed able to talk easy with people after that. I know I must seem inarticulate, but it's just I'm afraid still, and I'm only truly myself when I'm alone with Susan.

TRAINING HOMES

Training Home! What's that? I didn't ask the lady that took me. It was on a board outside of this big house. I remember it needed a coat of paint. The front of the house did too. And the curtains were the kind you couldn't see through, white cotton curtains, and I had to stand on tiptoe to look out at the street. She rang the door and my heart seemed to stop beating. The door was on a chain. I kept saying to myself 'Don't run.' But I wanted to run. And then the door was being opened and locked again behind us, and the key was on a chain which hung from her waist, and she was grey, everything was grey, from the veil round her head right down to her shoes, only they were black.

She seemed apologetic to the lady who had brought me. She apologized for the snow and the cold. 'I'm Sister Franklyn,' she said. She didn't look at me, so I didn't answer. I don't think she was telling me. Sister Franklyn seemed sorry that the hall was cold, and said to come into the sitting-room – tea was ready and there was a nice big fire, and I thought of feeling the warmth of that fire. Nearly all day we'd been travelling in her draughty little car from Exeter in Devon to Derbyshire. It was January, and snowing, and I was frozen stiff. But she didn't mean me. I stood there, just outside of the sitting-room. The table was laid for tea. I could see the fire for a moment as she held the

door open, and I could feel the heat of it. 'Come this way' –
and I was in a big room, a dirty brown room, with two long
brown tables and an even browner round one. And she said
'Sit down. One of the girls will bring you something,' and
she left me. I don't know why I didn't run. I thought of it.
I may even have started to make for the door, when it
opened. A girl came in. Her apron was filthy, and she had
another coarse one over the top, a brown canvas one; it
was soaking wet. I remember her arms were red and raw.
She looked very old, and yet she wasn't much older than
me. She had a white cap on, and her hair looked as if it
had been chopped off. She put a tray down on the table.
It was rusty, and there was only a pile of mashed potato
on it. We had not eaten all day. It was nearly four o'clock
in the afternoon, and they could only think of mashed
potato and a cold drink. I wanted to take it and smash it
at the wall and smash it at them or even at the girl who
brought it on her rusty dirty tray, and I was glad, yes glad,
that instead of kissing my mother good-bye I had spat in her
face, and I want to do the same to any other mother that
doesn't care what's happening to her child.

A FRIEND OF THE FAMILY*

The little room was very hot. I was sticky with heat and
had stripped off my nightdress. If I arched my back and
stretched my neck back, I could look through the window
just above. It was dark, and there were a lot of stars out.
I like to see the night. I was half awake, dreaming. But I
was suddenly very awake. There was just the suggestion of
a squeak. I didn't take much notice. Houses do squeak in

* This is the incident Pat had touched on earlier (see Chapter 3 and
Chapter 5). She was fourteen, he was thirty-five. It happened in her sister's
house.

the night. But then it was nearer, outside of the door. I remember I eased my back down, brought my head back to stare at the door, and I was stiff laying there waiting.

I know why I didn't scream. No one's told me – I know it. Before they do anything, good or bad, I'm frightened of them. And he took advantage of that fear, not of me. And it was the pain that might make me scream, that's what he thought. If she can just stay like that long enough, before she realizes, it will all be over; I can slip away. I didn't scream. I just cried. It's all been over a long time.

Chapter Seventeen

THE CONCERT

We were in the scullery, and the excitement was intense. We were jostling each other for the mirror, pushing and shoving to fix our clowns' costumes and put on our false noses. 'Hurry up you three – let the concert begin!'

We were sober now, quiet. My big sister looked at us two younger ones. 'Ready?' A big sigh. 'Yes, ready.'

We bounded through into the living-room, and went straight into the routine we had rehearsed – a song called 'Arm in Arm Together'. I was alto. We harmonized well, and our audience of three were spellbound. I felt it. We were a success.

It was my turn then to say my poem. 'I Wandered Lonely As a Cloud . . .' I was saying it with tears, and inside I was trying to tell them I'm lonely now, in spite of the song and the dancing, in spite of the way I make you laugh, I'm lonely. It was late and our little show was over. We thanked them politely for the sixpence and the special Friday night treat of fish with our chips. 'Good night Mum. Good night Dad. And good night to Dad's friend.'

'Good night girls, you're very good. Who knows, one day you may be famous!' Dad's friend told us.

We giggled as we went up to bed. 'Silly thing. We're not that good. We never will be without proper lessons.'

I cartwheeled over the end of the bed. My sister was still doing her act.

'Quiet up there. Blow out the candle, and get to sleep!'

I looked up at the ceiling, and screamed. There was that man!

In the morning they explained it was just the reflection of the tree outside of the window. 'You buy a blind, mother.' 'Yes father, that's best. But perhaps it was the fish . . . you never can tell.' I picked up my skipping rope and went out to play. I was still trying to think if they were right.

MY DREAM

I was very unhappy at this time. Richi was in prison on remand for murder, and I was desperate to get him the best help I could. I was living with a man who I had at first thought I might marry, mostly for security for Susan, and because I at one time was worried that she might feel she was different from other children, not having a father.

When Richi was taken away, he* changed completely, and became a drunkard and a gambler. I tried desperately to cling on to my first impression of him, but then realized he was making me ill, and I needed at that time to be at my strongest for Richi's sake and Susan's.

This man was not working. He was living off me, although I needed every penny I could scrape together in order to help Richi, and I came to hate him.

He had been drinking, and I had gone to bed feeling desperately unhappy. I couldn't sleep properly at this time, only fitfully, and must have dozed off for just a few minutes, but in my dream I clearly saw a child's coffin. It was lined with mauve silk, and although I could not see a child lying there, I knew it was Susan. I do not know why I was so sure, I only know no one could have told me differently; no one can now, and I live in constant fear of this happening.

I awoke at this point and remember only this feeling of terror and the need to tell someone, but I could not turn in any given direction and bumped into the wall several

* The man she was living with.

times, and in the end my legs wouldn't hold me up any longer and I fell to the floor in a stupor.

DREAMS

Patterns affect me very much indeed, especially kaleidoscopic patterns, and any which I may have seen on television during the evening, or in books, or even puzzle patterns which I may have looked at in my daughter's comic, seem to intrude into my dreams at night. I cannot look at moving patterns, except kinetics, some of which I find very restful.*

Other patterns I find very disturbing, and yet compelled to watch. I seem to be aware I am losing control of my senses, and have sometimes been so disturbed by patterned dreams that I am afraid to leave my bedroom window open; but they seem to affect me as much when I am awake as when I am asleep.

I dreamed the other night of two huge black cauldrons in a very dirty oven which contained a doughy substance which had spilled over and was running down the sides of the pots, and yet when I pushed it down with my hands the cauldrons seemed to contain only water.

I have what seem like photographic dreams where I see people as if in a picture. These people never speak and always appear very sad. They are always sat about as they would be if in a room.

The first of these dreams was during or after Richi's trial. It was so vivid that I could see the colour of the clothes and the texture and colour of their hair.

I can recall this photograph to mind (in fact it is printed

---

* I asked Pat more about this, and she said Brian Robbins did an exhibition of kinetic art – 'they weren't big and stark, and they went into pretty flower-like patterns'.

on my memory) at any time, and I know who the people are and why they look so sad. At first it distressed me, because I have a deep affection for them, but I am beginning to think that it is foolish to try and change one's destiny and that what has to happen very often will happen. I hope I can always live by this belief and not waste any more of my time in useless grieving.

In my dream I ran in terror from this dirty kitchen and stumbled up some steps into another room which was familiar to me, but the door on the right which I expected to find was sealed up, and a new door had been let into the opposite wall. I remember thinking I must get used now to opening the door with my right hand. I was aware of two voices talking, and one was Leila Berg's. The next morning I received from Leila a letter which upset me. I realize now it was something she felt she should write but that which, because of my deep regard for her, I had not thought she would think it necessary to write.*

I wonder if dreams do have any significance on our lives, and if so why they are not easier to understand. Is there also some sort of telepathy between people closely linked in some way. This dream was one which came during the writing of this book with Leila Berg.

GOOD-BYE MUM

I am not looking back. It is happening again. It is just plain fact, not adding to it.

I opened my eyes and looked around the bedroom. I was feeling tired still. I never seem able to wake refreshed, and

* My letter, which followed my initial talk with Pat about writing this book, said I hoped I hadn't led her to think it would *definitely* be published, and that it would 'change her life' and Richi's; it was a try, only.

yet when I do get up I can be dressed and out of the house in five minutes flat.

The morning I'm talking about was a long time ago now, but I cannot seem to forget it. Our bedroom was neat and clean, and I shared it with my two sisters Eileen and Grace.

This morning seemed different somehow. I felt uneasy. And my sisters were gone downstairs. I was disappointed. We usually had a pillow fight before going down to breakfast. Everyone seemed to avoid looking at me when I went into the living-room. I couldn't understand why they looked so furtive, and wondered what was wrong.

Breakfast was the usual weekday breakfast of porridge, toast, with jam or marmalade, with big cups of tea. No one seems quite so jolly during that breakfast. Usually we girls would argue a little as all sisters do and laugh a little, but this morning no one seemed to want to join in my conversation.

My mother said 'If you've finished your breakfast, come and wash,' and I washed in the big scullery which led off from the kitchen. I loved the smell of carbolic soap and I can smell it now as I write about this.

There was a knock on the door and I caught a glance between my elder sister and my mother, and my mother's face seemed paler than usual, and I felt that feeling of uneasiness again.

There was some talk, but I didn't hear it. I had heard only one sentence from my mother, and that was 'You are going away for a little while.' That was told to me only minutes before I walked down the steps to our front gate – 'You are going away for a little while!'

No one had to tell me that I would not be returning for a long time. I knew already. I knew that any member of any family that could do this terrible thing did not deserve, should not expect, to see me again. My mother said 'Won't you kiss me good-bye?'

I spat in her face.

I loved her then. I love her now. But except for a few short minutes when we could not find any words to share between us, I have never seen her again.

'Have you any idea why you were sent away, without a word of warning?' I asked Pat.

'I don't know,' she said. 'I've thought about it over and over. Sometimes I thought maybe it was because I came home late, but I only did it once, because I was so terrified of being late. It was right out of the blue. I wasn't taken to court or anything – I can't understand it. Could they do this to you – just send you away?

'I was fourteen years old.'

Chapter Eighteen

AIR RAID – HOLLOWAY PRISON 1940

The siren wailed and the door was unlocked and thrown wide. I jumped off the bed, expecting to be told to follow someone somewhere. I heard girls running. I groped my way to the cell door. 'What's happening?' I called out. 'It's a raid. You get unlocked during air raids.' I was aware of someone coming towards me. 'Can I come in with you, dear?' I couldn't see her clearly but she seemed older. We both sat on the bed, and she started to talk. She had two little girls. Her husband was looking after them, but she wasn't sure he would stay faithful. He might have left them to go with a woman. The children were nine and ten. I held her head in my arms and tried to comfort her. She was doing three months for shoplifting. Another girl was silhouetted in the doorway. She seemed younger, very sure of herself. She swore as she bumped into something, then sat down on the other side of me. She started to put her hands round my shoulder and then she seemed to be reaching for my breast. I moved away just as another girl burst in. It was the girl I'd met in reception. She'd just got back from her own personal raid on the aliens' quarters. 'I've just pinched a fruit-cake,' she told me. She broke off big chunks and gave some to all of us. It was very rich. It struck me that someone had made it in time for Christmas. It reminded me of Christmas at home. Then she chuckled and told me how it was hidden in a baby's crib. Somehow I didn't fancy the cake any more.

The All Clear had sounded hours ago and I was still very much awake and troubled by my own private thoughts.

The Train Back

BORSTAL FASHION. IT'S A RAID

It's a raid. Girls would start hammering on their doors. All hell seemed to be let loose. They weren't really frightened – it was just a chance to make a noise. There were cat-calls and swear-words, and a lot of laughter. I'd struggle to tie up my bed-roll, Borstal fashion. The door would open, and the screw would be there, caught with her hair down, wearing plaid dressing-gown, carpet slippers, the lot. It amused me to find them being motherly and calling us by our Christian names. We would fall over each other in our race downstairs, and my bed-roll usually opened out like a parachute at the top of the stairs. I always collapsed with laughter, and my stomach would ache every time we went through with this crazy charade, because the moment we were safely tucked into the cells below they would come along checking off our names and lock us up again.

REMANDED TO HOLLOWAY

The policeman threw open the cell door. 'Get up!' He said, 'You're leaving for Holloway in half an hour.'

'Where's that?' 'It's a woman's prison in London.'

I washed my face and combed my hair. Then he took me to a room off the cells, where a man and a woman were waiting. 'This is Sergeant Lowthorpe and this is his wife. Don't give them any trouble. They'll be escorting you by train. Don't give them any trouble. You'll find Mrs Lowthorpe a very nice woman.'

I looked at Mrs Lowthorpe. She was all dressed up in her Sunday best. I thought, just like Mum.

I sat on the bench while the sergeant was getting his last instructions – tickets, expenses, 'Oh, here's your sandwiches.'

The bobby who had brought my meals and stood guard while I washed pushed past. 'You off then?' The sergeant was telling me I had no property to sign for; I hadn't come with anything.

The sergeant's wife sat down. She seemed anxious I should like her. She started to tell me about her daughter-in-law. 'I'm a mother. I understand what you're going through. Our son has disappointed us, his father and me.' She looked at her husband as if it was something too terrible for him to bear. I wanted not to hear this terrible thing her son had done, but she was still talking. 'He married a girl from the fair-ground,' she said, as if it was the only thing that had ever touched her. I felt very sick.

Chapter Two The Journey

We had arrived at the station. It was foggy and cold, and one week to Christmas. 'All stations to Liverpool Street.' I was bundled on to the train. The door slammed, and I looked up to find nearly all the seats were occupied. I felt very self-conscious. I had expected we would have a carriage to ourselves. After two weeks in a local police cell seeing hardly anybody, it gave me a shock.

There wasn't room to sit together. The sergeant muttered something to a soldier. The soldier leaned forward, then seemed sorry he'd done it. His eyes flicked up. We stared at each other. Then he shuffled along a bit, and we both sat down. I was glad to have the seat by the window. The train gathered speed. My hand reached out for the door catch. I felt a grip on my wrist. The sergeant changed seats. I wished I hadn't done it. I love trains when I have a seat by the window.

The soldier got off at the next stop. He put his arm over the door to turn the handle. His eyes caught mine. He seemed to be saying something. I felt he was sorry for me. I hoped he wouldn't die. I hate wars. A dirty stinking mess, a war is.

Chapter Three Reception

We were taken into a big hall. The floor was grey stone. Round the wall were these lockers. They looked like over-size filing cabinets with just a seat inside. The seat had a ridge. I thought it might have a lavatory pan underneath. I remember trying to pull the seat up. Some girls were screaming, some just blaspheming. I thought of the din, and how cold I was. The door opened, and an officer handed me a mug of cocoa. I put both hands round the mug to warm them, and remembered how we all drank cocoa round the fire at home. How long ago was it?

A girl next to me was crying for her mother. Someone banged against her door. 'Shut up in there!' The door opened again. 'Strip to the waist, and wait to be called. You next for the doctor.'

Then I was in the bath, and a prisoner was standing by the door. She was watching me all the time. 'Can't you wait outside?' I asked her. 'No, I've got to see you wash properly.' I thought, what a job! 'Right. Time's up. Get your shoes over there by that table. You might get a pair to fit you – if you're lucky.' What a pile. I'll never find my size. I was aware of a girl my age pushing and shoving. 'You on a Borstal report?' 'Yes.' 'You don't have to wear prison clothes. Not if you don't want to.' I looked at the prison dresses. 'They'd fit me like a night dress.' We grinned at each other. 'Come on. Let's catch up with the others,' she said. I felt almost happy.

Pat

'I'll get you, my girl. Just you wait.' The woman was staring at me as if her eyes would pop out of her head. Her lips were almost curled back from her teeth, and she was puffing out puffs of breath. Her hands gripped her hips tight and her knuckles were all white.

I felt like I did when I was at home, and playing racing in our street, waiting for someone to say 'Get set – Go!' That's how I felt now, everything pounding inside of me, and waiting for my mind to say 'Go.'

'You told me to do it,' I said. But even then I was doubting my words. 'Told you? You little fool! As if I'd tell you to do a thing like that!' Her hand was shaking as she pointed to the hollyhocks, all neatly laid in a line on the flagstones.

The other girls had stopped working. Suddenly I was aware of every face looking at me. Some girls seemed to think it was a big joke. I choked down a giggle that had started to come up into my throat. Oh Christ, don't laugh!

I looked round harder at the faces. Some made me feel angry. They seemed so glad I was in trouble. I hate people who only feel up when someone else is down. And some seemed to be saying, 'Don't feel bad. We could easy have made that mistake. It could have been one of us.' It's easier if it's me. I can't bear other people's suffering.

She was yelling again. I turned round, and looked back at her. The nuns were behind her in the doorway. I caught a quick glance of those thick black stockings as they stepped over the door-sill. I licked a bead of sweat off my top lip. It had earth mixed with it, and it grated on my teeth.

She smiled. She was freshly laundered. Her face was laundered and made up. Her dark hair was curled neatly round her nursing-sister's cap, and her apron was like she'd been a few minutes before, but stiff with starch not anger.

The nuns started to move forward. As if she had suddenly remembered them she made a little dart ahead of them. 'This is Mary,' she was saying. 'This is Phyllis. A very good worker.' I stood petrified, wondering what she'd say about me. Their smiles were still on their faces as they passed through the gate into the convent.

I knelt down by the hollyhocks. How could I have made such a mistake? I looked at the bloom as it lay on my hand. It was very wilted. All those beautiful colours already fading. It's such a tall strong flower, I couldn't believe it would look so frail in death.

Pat told me, she had dug up a whole row of hollyhocks in bloom, at this Home – 'and yet my father had an allotment, and grew flowers to make money, and I worked on it. I *knew* you didn't take up flowers when they were in full bloom, so why did I do it?'

'Perhaps that was why,' I said, '. . . you remembered home.'

Chapter Nineteen

'Pat, what you wrote about the iron cots – was this something you have only just remembered?'

'Yes. I've never had that come into my memory before. This is something I've never known before. At Tony's, when his sister was playing the piano, I felt something coming back; and when I went to the exhibition and saw the cots, it clicked. I've been arguing with myself, "But I never was in hospital." But I must have been. No one has ever talked to me about this; I think I must have lost my memory completely about this. All the other things I have told you, I knew I had been forcing them out of my mind because I didn't want to remember. But this I didn't even know existed.'

'And these red flashes you talk about here – do you still have them?'

'Yes, I get them still a lot. It frightens me, but I push it out of my mind. It doesn't come at any particular time . . . when I'm looking at a railway poster . . . anything . . . I can even catch it out of the corner of my eye. Yesterday I went over to Susan Robinson. I was on the station. It was only just a tree. I caught it out of the corner of my eye, and I said to myself, "Don't look." Once, when I was being driven through a wood, I was frightened by the shapes of the trees too. I've never told anyone, only you. I love all trees, but some affect me in a terrifying way. Those tall thin ones with a smooth grey trunk . . .'

'Then when your brother said "Don't scream, or they'll send you away again",* maybe he was talking about this stay in hospital . . . do you think?'

* The incident on p. 41, that Pat suddenly remembered much earlier.

'Yes, maybe, that hospital where they had the iron cots. But when he said it, I didn't know about it.'

We went on talking about what she had written, Pat answering my questions.

'When I was fourteen, the first time I was sent away I was sent to my sister in Bournemouth, and when I came back my mother said, "Ooh, we've had some terrible scandal! You remember Mr Collander across the road? Well, he's been arrested for molesting some little girls!" I wanted to laugh . . .

'I realize now that my sister must have been terrified to say she'd gone on with her husband and left me with this other man, when she was about twenty-five and should have been responsible. So she'd never said anything. Let everyone think I'd run away with this man Frank . . .

'When I came out of those Homes, in the end, I was eighteen. Then my mother came to see me. (She did come while I was in Derby, but all I did was cry and my mother and father said nothing at all. So the Sister said "You'd better go.") It was in Ealing, when the Hereford people had got me a job in Ealing in service. They'd took me to the station, and put me on the train, and I watched the stations go by, and then it stopped at Swindon, and I thought "Oh. I'm going home!" And I started to get out. And there was my father! And he pushed me back into the carriage, and he said "Oh no you're not getting out. You're not coming home my girl. I'm taking you on to London."

'He took me to a hostel. Then I went to this job. One night, suddenly, my mother came with Auntie. We said "Hello", and I made them a cup of tea. I gave them two cold sausages from the larder. Her hair was pretty, permed, and she had a fur coat on. I kept saying "You do look nice." That was all. I suppose I was waiting for her to say "When are you coming home?" But it didn't seem to matter. Nothing did. Except that she was prettier – that mattered;

I was glad. I thought, perhaps it was because we were all grown up, and she had time to herself.

'She used to make all our clothes, Mum did. My father used to have to mend all our shoes, and he kept all this garden going for fruit and greens, and he used to sell a lot of flowers. He was a hardworking man. He had a shed where he used to work and he was always doing something.

'I used to groom my father's greyhounds, picked the fruit for puddings, and the peas, you know. But I was afraid of him, always apprehensive when he come in. He was a bit uncouth, not in his speech, but not gentle, you know.

'My mother used to make all our clothes, and unpick old ones to make them fit us – she made them nice – and my big sister used to knit our gloves. We had to go to church and Sunday school regular, but she never went and nor did my father. My brother was seventeen and the priest came round and said he hadn't seen him in church the last fortnight, and she said he'd got to go; but *she* never went.

'I remember being baptized. I remember getting a bunch of violets from the priest. I must have been seven or eight. I don't know why she took so long to baptize me. Perhaps it was because I was in the hospital before then . . . perhaps she didn't have me as a baby . . . because I don't remember any time before I was seven or eight.

'Sundays we went to church in the morning, Sunday school in the afternoon, church at night. It was Anglo-Catholic High Church. That's why I thought I'd get into trouble with playing with Denny, because he was Low Church, a plain little brick place without idols and things. It was a big church. The Sunday school was like a big school, with classrooms and a proper stage, and a convent where the nuns lived. In the week, we used to go up to the mission where the nuns were – there was a sewing class, and learning the plays, and that.'

'Weren't there good things too?'

'Oh yes. When I was in the swamps or on the sand-dunes alone, or when I was doing a play, or at the table when my mother was cooking and preserving things . . . all the lovely smells . . .

'I've never been able to remember something and talk about it to order like other people do. I think that's why I was afraid to mix with families, because they had things to talk about, tales to tell, and I couldn't recall anything.

'Sunday nights we'd all go for a long walk in the country and then he'd go into the pub and we'd all have a lemonade in the pub garden.

'She was very respectable and refined, my mother. My mother and father would sometimes discuss politics at meals, and I used to listen.

'The Welsh miners, starving men, walked through the town. And my mother said to my father "Did you see *that rabble*?" I couldn't understand – she could only just hold her head above water – how could she talk about them like that? These things worried me as a child. She should have been out sharing her things with them, giving them food as they passed. If I can feel it and I'm just a kid, why can't grown-up people feel it?

'I never saw any emotion on my mother's face. Except on Friday when she saw how much money she had to manage on. Every Friday she used to cry. I used to think, "This time I'll go out and not see it." But somehow I always stayed.

'We played indoors. The post office was the chair back to front. And we had dressing-up clothes. But sometimes my father came back with this man, and we used to get up out of bed to do a show for him. I used to do a parody of my Mum with very exaggerated posh accent. Everyone else used to think it very funny but I often wonder if my mother used to be a bit disappointed since she was an opera fan. I didn't do it maliciously . . . that was how it came over to me. She used to go to the operatic theatre every week with the lady next door. I used to say to her, "Sing me a number, sing me a number." And she used to sing, "I'll See You Again" . . . or "We'll Gather Lilacs in the Spring Again". I liked more earthy stuff. So when we did our shows I used to get a feather boa, and pad out my chest, like I imagined these singers to be. Maybe it was my sense of humour my mother didn't like, I don't know.

'In Borstal there were so many Pats, we used to have to make our own names up, to be an individual. So they called me Jackie. There was a girl there with a beautiful operatic voice, and I laughed. And I remember I had to explain to the girl because she was very upset. Later I listened to her enthralled . . .

'I walked out of that service job in Ealing. I was only there a few months. I just walked out of it one night and never went back. I was very unhappy. It was a few nights after my mother had visited me that I left. All she said to me on that visit was she was glad to see me happy and in a nice job. It was as if she was so sure that this was where I should be, and she was so wrong – and that was why I had to show her. I was crying all that night in bed. I couldn't get it out of my mind. I was thinking "How dare she! How dare she think this was what I should be doing! Just cleaning up after somebody else. How dare she!" . . . It was the sort of job all my sisters ended up doing, except that they gradually moved out into Lyon's Corner House. Yes, I think she was quite happy to think she'd produced five future housemaids – servants. When I was very little and listened to her talking, I knew that this was what I was supposed to become, and I was terrified to grow up and become a housemaid. I think perhaps part of me refused to grow up, still is refusing to grow up, because I haven't done what I want to do, and be what I want to be – and I *will* be it, or die. I don't owe myself to anybody any more –

that's how I feel. That's not how I want to feel – I'm fighting it the whole time – but that's how I feel!

'So I walked out, I walked and walked. I was on the road all the time. I suppose we were the first of the Flower People . . . young people who were stuck in lousy jobs they couldn't stand and ran away out of protest. We didn't always have shoes on our feet, and we were dirty and unkempt; but it wasn't a deliberate form of dress. I got food where I could, or I starved. I never thought of asking anybody, but sometimes people offered help, even if it was only a meal. And the rest of the time I was lost in the beauty of the countryside. I wasn't terribly sad. I roamed round like that for two years, till I went to Borstal. I became cunning, because I learned pretty early on that people didn't care if you were starving, but it brought some reaction if you were starving and dirty. I met people whom I was interested in, but not anyone who was interested in me. I wanted to know how. I wanted to know why, why people were wandering. But people didn't like me asking them. They shied away from me. They congregated together, but they were nervous of me. I want to ask everyone *why*. I'm interested in people. Animals interest me too – if you sit long enough and quiet enough, somewhere where you're completely alone, they're nearly as fascinating as people – they're finding out all the time.

'Even when I was wandering about with no fixed abode, I wasn't bothered at being alone. It may have bothered other people, but it didn't bother me . . . because I could escape into a park or a wood and watch a squirrel. I think people should do this more, watch any living creature. But to be a cabbage – that is dangerous. That's what that doctor said to me – "Don't be a cabbage!" I laughed. I was a child, and it was funny. But I know now what he meant. And I think that's the part I've always remembered. I've never been a cabbage in my mind. My mind is my own. I may look like a cabbage, but I'm not inside my head.

'Why did I marry my husband? Well, in Borstal there were always crowds of people when you wanted them. And now on this farm I only had two elderly people. And as this chap was chasing me round the woods . . . I think I thought he was a serious person and I would learn from him, but he wasn't serious – he was just withdrawn. I thought when I wanted to know about important things he would be able to tell me, but he couldn't . . .

'I was still in the bath when I should have been halfway to the registry-office, and there was this banging at the door – "What are you doing!" If no one had bothered to come back, I should have probably forgotten the whole thing.

'After I'd been married six years I admitted to myself that there was something seriously wrong with him. Then it was a case of getting doctors to see it.

'When I first met him, we used to discuss religion. He talked with intensity about religion, and I thought he was thinking about it; but later I came to see he wasn't thinking, he was repeating over and over again, but only to himself. Because I was so ignorant, and couldn't talk, it took me a long time to realize he didn't have any conception of religion – he was just a record with the needle stuck, going over and over. And then I knew I shouldn't marry him.

'I went through with the marriage only for one reason – I had to escape. I had to get out to London. I thought there might be a chance for me there, that there I could do the things I wanted to. I know it was a childish act, to think you could marry just in order to escape. It's stupid. But up to then I'd been able to do it, to walk out of jobs, to run away, and I thought I could still do it.

'We didn't go out. He didn't mix with people, and he

didn't want me to either. We did have dramas,* but they were indoors. They were impossible situations that I couldn't cope with. Even now I can't talk about it, but I think I can write it.

'I had a dream the other night. My husband was lying on the bottom end of the bed, with his feet on the floor. I rushed to the door to get away, but though I knew I had time to do it, yet I couldn't open it.

'He had a lot of control over me. He still, in hospital, talked to me about the murders, describing in absolute detail just where they were all buried ... five-bar gates, how many steps ... (He always liked country things. He may have been terribly disappointed about that, because he wasn't anybody who liked a lot of noise, and I think he expected his father's farm to come to him; but they sold it.) And that I'd allowed police into the farm to search it ... and that he didn't have me and Richi, he had "a wife and a little daughter".

'In fact, he became even more demanding. And I was frightened to ignore the things he said and just see them as part of his illness – if he said I'd got to bring him a new shirt, I thought I'd *got* to bring him a new shirt – I didn't dare come without it. And at last it came to the point where he wouldn't even accept me. We had two hours together, every Thursday and every Sunday, and I'd keep ordering cups of tea – I didn't know what else to do – and now and then he'd leer and say "Well, we won't have that one, the one you've put the poison in."

'I couldn't accept that he wasn't capable of relating Thursday, visiting day, to me, that he was too much removed from reality for that. I was afraid I was putting more pressure on somebody that was already ill – would I make him worse by not going? All I thought was that he was there by having worried himself into being ill. (Nobody

* She was thinking back – in joke – to her childhood play-actings.

130

explained to me about schizophrenia . . . or maybe they did and I didn't understand.) And that I might worry him by not coming, and make him worse . . .

'I was always under his thumb. I had never dared to disagree with him. He felt himself much above me intellectually. I married him because I thought he would help me grow, but he didn't; he seemed to want to push me down more. But I just accepted it. I didn't feel strong enough to stand up against him. The only time I showed any fight was when I thought he was too harsh to Richi. He didn't know how to play with Richi, and resented me reading a bedtime story to Richi – he'd never had anything like that with his mother, though he had from this old woman they'd retained to help with the housework. But I didn't give in on this; I thought it was a kid's right to have something like this. He didn't give Richi any time at all. I don't think Richi has any memory of his father at all, and that's why I don't like to talk to Richi about him.'

(I said 'He does.' I told Pat what Richi had said to me in the Scrubs . . .)

'It's true about him chasing me round the kitchen while I had Richi in my arms . . . I ran out with him . . . But he was very little . . . No, no one could have told Richi about that; he must really have remembered it . . .

'His relations are so very ignorant, that I was terrified they would say a lot to Richi. They'd exaggerate and distort beyond reason. The trouble they went to, to establish that *I* was mad! . . . His sister was kind, and wanted to help; but she didn't know any more than me, only rather than say nothing she'd imagine things to say.

'He'd been very ill as a child, he'd been in hospital for years. He didn't start school till he was eleven. His sister used to come to the hospital with me, at first, to see him and give me support, but he couldn't bear her. He'd say

"What are you here for?" I was very torn – I wanted to
have a relaxed visit, and yet I wanted her support. Apparently she burned him on the back of the hand with a hairpin
when he was little.

'He couldn't have had a happy childhood because his
mother allowed this woman to become his unofficial foster-
mother. He had this operation as a child, that it was
apparently an amazing thing for a grown man to get
through. It was talked about a lot at the time. She used to
have to take him up for conferences of eminent people
where they discussed him, because it was supposed to be so
remarkable that he survived it. Well, I don't believe he
survived it; I think he paid for it when he became mentally
ill. It was in his guts; he was fed through tubes for God
knows how long. Apparently there was a big thing once
when they decided he could have some solid food, and
when it came it was two tiny squares, stamp-size, of bread
and butter, and he went berserk and attacked the nurse, and
they had to give him an injection and God knows what.
He was twenty-seven and he'd never had a girlfriend. His
mother, when she was first talking about him saying he'd
be down for the week-end, and I asked what he was like,
she said "Oh, he hates women." They talked as though
he'd never been out with a girl. Whether it was that he
never told them anything, or whether it was true, I don't
know.

'I went to see him one time. He was up. They sit them
about in armchairs. He had been expecting me. He was in
a locked ward. Just as the nurse was unlocking the door to
let him out I was – luckily – already at the door of the ward.
He rushed at me shouting "I'll fuck you in the meadow!
I'll fuck you in the meadow!" He chased me round and
round the ward yelling "I'll fuck you in the meadow! I'll
fuck you in the meadow!" Everyone was standing there
looking horrified and appalled. Every time we came past

the Sister I called out, "He doesn't usually use language like this, Sister!"*

'As a matter of fact, he really *didn't* normally use language like that. He was a very quiet studious chap, always studying technical books; the only outdoor activity he ever did was fishing!

'They had to get a doctor to him, and give him an injection.

'What made me have to go into hospital myself last year? I don't know! Maybe it was the thunderstorm the night before. It was a terrific storm. I was terrified, but I had to hide it from Susan. This is the only practical reason I can find, because in fact we were happier and more relaxed at that time than we'd ever been.

'Every part of me itched. I kept running my hands under the cold tap, kept getting into cold water and getting it over my body. My heart was beating very fast – and this happens now, sometimes for no reason, and it frightens me. I think there must be something wrong with me – but I don't dwell on it. I don't dwell on any of these things. In bed at night, when I'm drowsy, not dreaming, I get these heart-beatings. And I hear voices. I don't mean voices like someone mentally ill, I mean instead of a dream . . . No, I don't listen to what they are saying. I think I've been too frightened to. But now that you said you've had this too, and that they may be saying something important, I think I'll listen to them, like you say . . .

'I was ill, you see, at night-time. I thought I'd run and get someone, Nancie or Mrs Ardizzone, and come back with them and wrap Susie up in a blanket. I didn't know what was wrong. I just had this terrible feeling. I ended up the street police station, actually. Perhaps being in there with all the policemen there, I started screaming and calling them all sorts of names. They got an ambulance, and I

* Pat is very good at telling stories. She had me crying with laughter.

managed to write down my address, and I kept saying "The baby, the baby"; and they said "Don't worry. We'll send a policewoman to look after her." And of course I thought they would. At the hospital my doctor said I'd be better at home because of the baby, so they said they'd send me home. I didn't really want to go home, I felt so ill, but I wanted to because of the baby. And I'll never forget coming back in the ambulance – right down the street you could hear the baby screaming! There wasn't anyone with her at all! She'd wakened up and found me gone and was running all over the house looking for me. I always remember the ambulance men looking at each other and saying "Well, what are we supposed to do? Leave them like this?" And then they drove off. And Susie and me we cuddled each other and settled down to sleep, me with all my clothes on. She's never forgotten it, never. You know how you say to a child, "I'm only in the kitchen. I won't be long." She says "But you were, you were."

'The next day when I woke up the same feeling was starting again. I had the baby with me and I was walking into the wall. I didn't seem able to walk straight. And her voice seemed to be coming from far away, and she was saying "Walk straight, Mummy!" And I think one of the people at the flats must have phoned for an ambulance because I just remember sitting by the new river with a crowd round me and the ambulance came and I went back to the local hospital. Then they must have got into touch with the Child Care and she went into the nursery and I went into Friern. I was there four weeks.

'People were on at me to come out because of Susan, and were almost imagining me to have withdrawn from the world, which I certainly hadn't – I wasn't withdrawn from the world in that hospital, by God! I wanted to *know* what had caused it. But I couldn't stay there.

'Susie was changed to a foster mother. I was worried

about it. You hear so much about foster mothers, some good, some bad. So I walked out of the hospital. Anyway I think you'd have to be totally incapable of reason to stay in those places long. When I picked her up, she was speechless for half an hour. It was very sad. It was terrible, because she really didn't understand anything. It must have been a terrifying experience for her, one minute to be secure, next minute people taking you away. I daren't think of it now really. Now, whenever she talks about it, I talk about it with her. She won't be put off, she wants to know, so I think the more I talk about it and explain, the better. I explain to her that someone said they'd come and sit with her, I didn't mean her to be left alone like that, and I promise it'll never happen again; and I mean that. There was twice – that night, and then again the next day. Sometimes I forget, and when she follows me around I say "My goodness, Susie, surely you can stay by yourself for just a minute." And then she says "But you left me." So I start again, explaining.

'Even last night, Susie and I were coming up the steps. She'd been staying with a friend. I said to her, "You've been quite happy with Pearl, haven't you?" "Yes. But you won't forget to come for me tomorrow after the nursery?" I said "Of course not. Why would I do that?" "Well you said you'd stay and have a cup of tea." "Well, of course. She'd looked after you, and naturally when I came she wanted me to stay for a few minutes." "But remember, last week (she always calls that time last week), when your bed was in the playroom, and I came to look for you and you weren't there . . .?" I think she thought I'd go to Pearl's tonight, and she'd say "Stay and have a cup of tea", and I'd say yes, and she thought I'd stay and be too late to collect her, and out of that comes the thought, as it always does, of what had happened that night.

'But the policewoman was in the hospital with me! It

was only when they'd given me a tablet to make me relaxed that I realized she was there, and I thought "My God, what's she doing here! She should be with Susie!"'

'It was a nightmare place that hospital. The worst thing was the unnecessary impatience. In wards like that, they're not constantly rushing about with very physically sick people, they have time to be kind, if they're the right sort of people. After all, if people who are sick can be kind to each other I don't see why nurses, who are supposed to be physically capable, can't be. I think doctors should be *aware* that nurses can be undermining whatever they do. After all, it's natural old people shouldn't take tablets because they're afraid they'll poison them or something; but the nurses don't care – they just say "Oh well, it's her affair, if she just doesn't want to get well . . ." And that's what *I* was doing – worrying myself sick to get patients to take what the doctor had told them!

'It was the same with me. There was I, not dangerous as far as I know to myself or anyone else, and this consultant psychiatrist saying over and over again I must get out into the fresh air. And the nurses refusing to let me out. I'd have gone right round the bend if I'd stayed there. In the end, I just walked out. I didn't know the result of anything – I had . . . one of those things where they put things in your head . . . something cardiograph. I had one at Whittington Hospital; they took me from Friern in an ambulance; but I never saw the results.

'All the time I was at Friern, the whole four weeks, I couldn't talk to anyone. I've been sent to dozens of psychiatrists and never been able to talk to anyone. It seems funny that this man years ago was so good and yet no memory of it remains to help me talk to one when I was grown up. I just can't talk to them. Nobody knows any of these things about me. They could be bloody dangerous but nobody knows.

'I can't talk – I can only write. I go into a trance when I write, and I know that the absolute truth is being shown to me. I am not aware of anything except being transported back in time, and everything is happening as if I was a child. The writing is automatic. First of all, it affects my stomach – it's tight and hurts, and that's the first instance I know I have to write. Then, whatever stage I'm writing, I am that age when I'm writing it, and whatever it's done to me at that time I'm feeling it, and experiencing again what I only experienced then *inside* of me (sometimes showing a different feeling outside). And when I've finished writing I'm sobbing maybe, or terrified.

'That's why if the style is childish, that's how I was then when I was writing. I want you to understand, so if someone says to you "It's written too childish", you can say "Well, it wouldn't be true if we wrote it all again in adult words and adult sentences. It would be fake." So don't you worry – I can't stop writing it now.

'I can talk to you about what's happening to me. But with the book, I have to go right back, and *feel* what happened, otherwise no one will ever know what really happened. I don't know what will come out of me, or when it will come out, but it *will* come out, because I just can't stop it now. And I've got to write about these things, because they're important to me. And I've got to write about them truthfully, just how they happened, or I won't know.

'With Dr Mayer,* I wasn't even aware of problems. I think he just wanted me to go – after Richi, you know – just so as I'd know he was at hand. If you aren't *aware* of the problems yourself, how can you talk about them? Unless there's some way of making you leave the world completely,

* Her G.P. – a kind, local man.

put you under hypnotism or something . . . isn't there a psychiatrist somewhere in the whole country who does this? Maybe there's millions of people who are falling by the wayside just because they can't accept the established things like shock treatment, insulin, and so on . . . maybe there are psychiatrists who are trying to get this accepted, and people say "It's dangerous." But my God, isn't shock treatment dangerous? I've seen people terrified of it. And my husband was terrified of insulin treatment.

'I went to hospital once with Richi. He was very fat and I thought he was going to be bandy. And the woman said "You seem upset. Why don't you see a doctor." And he gave me a letter to go to a clinic where there was a big psychiatrist . . . But it wasn't any use. I can't talk to these people. I could write it, I think, but they don't ask me.'

Chapter Twenty

I went round to see Pat. She had written down two more pieces.

BORSTAL BROWN

I think I went into Borstal determined to be a bloody nuisance. I think I was so disgusted by events after being arrested that I was glad to be there to give vent to my feelings without them being able to punish me any further.

It was at this time that I changed my name to Pat Gale. I didn't want my mother worried and couldn't bear to see her again, especially in those circumstances. So when they asked 'What's your name?' I combined my mother's surname and the Christian name of my niece, and there I was in that country police station reborn Pat Gale.

We were taken to Aylesbury in a big prison bus. 'Borstal girls in the front, prisoners in the back,' they said as we got in. There was some marvellous escape plan on, but I didn't get excited. I summed up the girl who did the arranging, and knew it was all just a figment of her imagination.

So one weary cold February night I lay in a cold dreary prison room and began without any interest or enthusiasm my Borstal sentence. A lot of boredom, a few laughs, and a bit of excitement could sum it up. And yet I want to tell this part of my story in detail.

Perhaps I'm interested to know how much it has all changed. Perhaps once a prisoner, always a prisoner. Well, I would like to think so. And I am interested to know if the odd balls, the girls who like me didn't seem to fit in, have got more chance to express themselves now.

The Train Back

Borstal then was geared to three stages. When you arrived, you were put in a prison wing, segregated as it were. I understand this still goes on today. In this first three months they were assessing you, apparently. It was such a load of balderdash that I just wouldn't play, and I got relegated to coal-carting, just that, all day long pushing barrows of coke from one tip to another. I liked it. I was out in the grounds. I was able to look up at the sky, feel the wind, even the rain. And the job was so repetitious I only required my hands and feet to do it – my mind was mine! I had a lot to learn. They didn't even want to leave me my mind.

After a day outside it was irksome to be taken back, given tea, and locked up at four-thirty in the afternoon. I couldn't believe this was possible, and I would sweat and fume for some sort of playtime to start, and for my door to be unlocked again. I would sometimes hear other doors open, and bang on mine, terrified I would be missed out. 'Miss! Miss!' 'Sorry Gale. You're not on the activity list tonight.' Activity! The bastards – what the hell is activity. 'I just want you to open that door!' I'd scream, and crash and bang with my pot against the door. Troublemaker? No. Just I had to protest against the stupidity of people who will accept any standards, or whose standards are so low even these places seem exciting or safe.

I thought of the prisoner back in Holloway who had said, 'Got a Borstal love? Don't you worry. It's a lovely place.' I thought, 'Is it me? Did she put up with this night after night, without any protest?' I felt guilty, as if perhaps you have to refit your mind or your personality before entering, and in my innocence of the prison system I had forgotten to do so.

I survived it, but only just. And except for one Borstal officer I thought they were crap then, and I still think of them as crap now – time has not mellowed me.

Pat

I tried desperately to let things ride, just as Smithy (that's what we called her) urged me to do. She would come to me on the punishment block, when I was on bread and water diet, and talk, low-voiced without emotion in it almost, but insistent, as if she didn't care a damn about whether I became head girl of Borstal – this was no finishing school – but only how I survived it. I learned to accept help from others. I wasn't quite such a loner.

The Governor will always remain in my memory as a monument to impotence. She was the most impotent woman I could ever meet. I pray that her kind are accidents of birth, and that women are not all like her in these sort of situations. I think of one colour when I think of her – brown, dark sludgy brown. Her face was expressionless, and when she spoke it was as if her assistant who was always with her was pulling a string. The mouth opened and closed, and it was expressionless. She was very tall, and thin to the point of emaciation, and she wore brown. Everything was brown. Her costume, stockings, and shoes. Even the powder she wore was brown. I used to think, ironically, she was trying to fit in, in some way, with the brown of our Borstal uniform.

Twelve months, fifteen months, two years went by. Girls came. Girls went. I used to joke and say 'I'll go on here for ever.' I carved my name deep on the punishment exercise wall. The screws would herd me through the iron gate and clang it shut behind me. Unless they pulled the wall down it must still be visible. And I carved it with pride.

I had not conformed, become a cabbage. I could see through to their very souls. It was why they hated me – they knew I could tell. I had the ability to tell, but they needn't have been frightened, I never had a chance to tell. Six months after leaving Borstal I was married, and within a year had protestingly and with a heart full of agony given birth to my son.

I had been reading with Pat's glasses on. I had left mine at home, and, half for a joke, had borrowed Pat's. By now, my head was splitting with eye-strain. I said, 'Can you bear to read the second one aloud, Pat?' So Pat began to read. Now her own voice was reading quite consciously and deliberately what she had written down in distress.

ABSOLUTELY MY EARLIEST RECOLLECTIONS

– I am six years old

This whole book has been a reliving of my life. The events may have taken place in many different places, but the reliving of it has been done in my flat, alone except for Susan, my four-year-old daughter, asleep on the settee.

It has been an unnerving experience, sometimes even terrifying. To be transported back in time into some unknown place and some different age in one's life, and not to be able to control it or stop it, is an unnerving experience. But I have always thought 'Why can't I ever remember beyond a certain age. Children can't be born at the age of eight. There must be something known to me about my earlier childhood.'

The book was nearly complete, the end in sight, and yet we had no beginning other than where I was born. We had talked about this, Leila and me. I had told her that I could remember nothing beyond a certain point, and on this particular night I was desperately trying to force some earlier recollection into my mind again. I became aware of seeming to go into some sort of trance, and then, incredible though it may seem to many people, I had become in my mind a child. I was unaware of my own familiar surroundings, and only conscious of being in a strange bed. Someone was tapping on my head and calling my name. I wanted to tap back. I was aware of wanting to speak or cry but my lips wouldn't move. I felt a pressure on my hand. I tried to look with my eyes but they refused to open. I accepted the fact that I was in a bed as if it was the only thing I had known.

I made a great effort and tapped back with my fingers on the hand that was holding mine. A voice said 'Open your eyes. You're not blind. Open your eyes.' I tried hard to open them. The voice seemed to come from far away, yet it was insistent. I wanted to communicate. I was desperate for companionship. I pressed urgently with my fingers against the palm of the hand, pressing each in turn slowly at first and then more quickly as if I was playing a piano. 'Play you a tune, is that it?' the voice asked me. I felt myself lifted up in strong arms and carried to a piano. A voice sang 'Ding Dong Bell' very loud, as if I were deaf as well as dumb, and while he sang he pressed my hands down on the keyboard. It must have stimulated some memory, and I pressed my fingers down with my own strength until he took his hands away from mine, and I was playing each note in turn, and suddenly aware that my eyes were open, my face muscles had relaxed, and I was smiling, and even making some noise with my mouth (which sounded like Pussy) every time he came to the line 'Pussy's in the well'. He played it over and over. I'm not trying to say it happened in a few moments. I'm sure I collapsed exhausted over the piano just as I did over the table, but I felt him ruffle my hair and whisper 'Tap on wood, Joanie, always tap on wood.' It was to become a sort of sign between us. In the months that followed, this doctor was to spend many hours with me, teaching me words, helping me to speak, to form the sounds, but – most important – to write, grown-up writing just like he did it; perhaps I wouldn't settle for less.

He told me my name, how old I was, how long I had been there. He told me I had one brother and four sisters. He told me I had a mother and father. But it meant nothing.

I stared back at him disinterested. Only two things could rouse my interest – when he played the piano or when he gave me pencil and paper.

I wrote, and wrote, and wrote. I made him show me how to put the stories I made up in my head, on paper. He helped me to write my stories. I realize now they were fantasies because I had no other experience of life except in that hospital bed. But because I couldn't leave off writing, I was the cause of getting him into trouble.

I used to pretend to be asleep if I heard his footsteps. I did now. But he wasn't alone. I don't know if I looked particularly haggard, but the other doctor with him seemed upset, and his voice was raised in anger, and what I now know as accusations were made about each other's methods. My doctor – I thought of him as my doctor – was thought to be over-taxing my strength. They were afraid I would relapse into what they had considered was a form of paralysis and of even damaging my brain permanently, and of using methods which were not acceptable.

He was defiant and brilliant in his own defence, and I listened and took in every word. I couldn't understand them all, but the drama of it was not lost on me, and the words rushed back at me while I was in this state of trance as if I was listening to a play. I was aware of how he had given me words to use, described their meaning, and the quiet of my flat was broken as I heard myself saying in a loud strident voice, 'I will defy you.'

I think that is what he did, for the sake of one skinny six-year-old kid – for me, all those years ago. I believe he defied convention because he believed so strongly that I was not mentally handicapped. I believe he risked his whole career to prove he could get me better, to prove I could be taught, that my brain was capable of learning and that I did have control over my senses.

I remember his intensity, how he kept urging me to keep

writing. 'People may hurt you, Joan,' he would say, 'but not the written word. Choose your way in life as much as you can. Stay away from people who give you too much to bear. Don't take on too many burdens. If you do this, there's a chance you'll make it.' I didn't understand every-thing then, and yet events have proved him right, and I hope there are doctors as brave as him, giving kids and grown-ups a chance when more orthodox methods have failed, willing to try as he did a new method. That method was hypnosis.

Everyone like me needs somebody special, or rather everyone like me who is born out of their element. I don't know who these people are. They must exist. Perhaps they have even yet to know it themselves. Perhaps this book will reach those people. The old rules don't apply to people like me, the old maxims, the old treatment. I don't mind being a suitable case for treatment, but I want the right sort of treatment. And I demand that great men of learning, yes even those who have reached the top of their profession, the consultant psychiatrists of this world should turn their eyes inwards, examine their hearts, and then see if they can still say so complacently, 'I can learn nothing more.' I say they can. I say they must. Or we might all just as well become the abortion of birth which God knows I wish sometimes even now that I had been.

By now, Pat was crying.

'So what is your name really?' I said.

'Joan Townsend.'

'And does nobody in London know?' I said.

'Nobody. Only you!'

So Pat Chapman was really Joan Townsend. And Joan Townsend had become Pat Gale who was called neither Pat nor Joan but Jackie, and who later became Pat

The Train Back

Chapman to signalize a relationship with a man who, having been a collection of tubes and the horizontal depersonalized object of conferences, became schizophrenic and could not make relationships, and who finally did not recognize her and told her she was dead and indeed had never existed.

Chapter Twenty-one

Now the writing came in very fluently from Pat, several pieces in each envelope.

THREE IN ONE

To Leila

I can't think why I never saw it before. There are two of them and me. It doesn't worry me because I stand apart from the other two. I listen to them talking. Sometimes I wonder if they are just teasing each other or if underneath it isn't much more sinister. One is more tolerant but she is self-educated and finds this hard to bear at times. They seem to have a great understanding for each other. It's the other one, I think, for who I have the most concern. She is such a child. The other one cannot always control herself, yet she can feel ashamed and I know hates it when she is mean. There is no doubt in my mind that they do love each other. I want her to succeed. It means in their own ways then they can both be happy.

P.S. I am not her. She is not me. We agree we are living within each other.

BROKEN DOLL

I hate to look at dolls that are broken or so misused that the paint is all washed away from the face, and the hair is gone lank and only tufts of it remain, the head no longer is joined firmly to the body and lolls backward when a child plays with it – a doll that is lifeless is a monstrosity. I once had to stand by and watch little children play with a doll like this for want of anything better. It stirred up in me an anger I couldn't control and a feeling of terror I didn't understand. No one understands because no one believes even now what I say – what I know. I cannot understand it myself but on that particular day when I made myself at last look at that doll full in the face I saw the doll but yet was convinced beyond all doubt that the death was Susan's. I can't explain it. I can't understand it. I have no one who can help me to understand it. I don't believe in premonition, and yet I know that every day that passes with my little girl is a day of joy and sorrow. I can't teach her enough the wonders of the countryside. I can't get enough of her love; it is as if I want to cram wonderful happy times into a few short years. I feel a desperate anxiety to take her to places of interest and to have her share the London that I love, and at the back of my mind I have this nagging doubt that there just isn't enough time.

Pat has been having to get up at night, to use the lavatory. She gets up very softly so as not to disturb Susie, and tiptoes with painful care down the dark corridor; but however hard she tries she is soon aware of a patter or a flicker behind her, and she turns and there is Susie, eyes almost closed in sleep, padding barefoot and silent behind her down the dark hall. Pat tells me about it, half laughing.

Perhaps a middle-class woman, who could go to a psychiatrist, who would have other people in the house to look after the child if she were to go to hospital, or who has relatives living tidily in declared places who could be called upon, would not find her child tiptoeing down the corridor behind her in the middle of the night. Perhaps she would not see little coffins in her dreams.

Pat

MY PEOPLE

I was in the ark. It was a self-contained punishment flat. I had my own hand basin and lav, and no real contact with the other girls until my stint of solitary confinement was over. After three days you were allowed a book to read.

My bed was a block of wood raised off the floor a few inches. Other than that the room was bare. I was stretched on my belly, trying to ease my aching backside. I heard the doors open and slam shut and footsteps. I automatically pulled myself into a sitting position. I had been in the ark enough times to know Borstal officers didn't like to see us resting while they were working. You would have thought they were working for free.

The door to my cell wasn't solid. Just bars from top to bottom. I felt like a monkey. An officer was unlocking the door.

'Tidy yourself up, Gale. Your people are here.' I let out a groan of agony. My people? I repeated it after her like an idiot. I had no people. I had them dead and buried in my mind. *I had no people.* I couldn't make any attempt to rise up off my wooden plank. She hooked her hand round my neck. 'Come on, Gale. Snap out of it!' And then I was up, rushing for the hand basin, splashing water in my face, groping for the towel, talking too loud, laughing and crying but pretending I had soap in my eyes. 'Where's your shoes, Gale?' 'My shoes?' We started to make an idiotic search of that bare room. 'You've got them somewhere, Miss. They don't let me wear them in here.' 'Oh damn. Sorry, Gale. They're in the cupboard.' They looked dusty. I got them on somehow, and rubbed them one at a time up the backs of my black stockinged legs. I was as tense as a steel spring. 'Let's go then,' she said, and we moved off. Unlock the

149

door, slam it shut, unlock the other door, slam it shut; we are in the main corridor.

The Saturday afternoon monkeys are having their free association. 'It's Jackie Gale.' I looked up and there are all the other monkeys clamouring at their gate, grinning from ear to ear. 'All right, Jackie. Someone asked you out for good. Glad to see you, Jackie.' I felt my guts uncoil. I grinned back. I put up my hand in salute, and we were through the side door. I breathed in the misty wintry damp air. I liked it. It could have been any sort of day. Our war was over. They had come. There was still the agony of our meeting to be got over but they were waiting for me up at the gate.

'Wait there. I'll see if the Governor is ready.' I sank on to the seat outside of the door. 'Oh no. Please God, let me go in by myself, as if nothing has happened. Just say "Hello Mum. Hello Dad!"'

'Gale!' I pushed myself up from the chair. I felt very very old. I was at the threshold of the room, and the Governor's impersonal voice was explaining. 'These people are willing to give you a job, to take you into their family. I will leave you alone to talk for a while.'

I moved into the room. I was aware of nothing. I turned towards them. They were strangers.

Chapter Twenty-two

TIME TO GO

I finally made it to special side. No point in keeping me locked up. I had accepted the job. They had accepted me.

I was working inside scrubbing floors. They were determined I would go out in the proper manner, that this time I would not slip out through the long grass.

'Gale!' I had been slopping water about with a cloth, making some pretence at scrubbing the floor, and I was very bored. 'Go with Johnson, and try to behave yourself.' I jumped up like a cat on hot bricks. Any excuse to get away from that damn scrubbing brush. The door clanged behind me and we were out and on our way round to the machine shop.

This girl, Johnnie we called her for short, was raving on about the civvy coat they were making me. I wasn't too interested, except that it had to be short because I liked them that way. All supplied by kind permission of H.M. Government.

I felt very self-conscious standing up on the table in front of all the girls, being pushed this way, pulled that way, while the coat was marked for darts and button-holes. She was a qualified tailoress outside, and was giving full vent to her artistic talents, and determined that everyone should see how good her talents were. It was a navy blue reefer coat, half belt, three quarter slit up the back. A navy blue serge dress to match with long sleeves, white silk collar and cuffs.

The collar and cuffs were an added touch of her genius, and a farewell gift. She had wangled the silk and got permission from the machine room officer to make them for me.

She motioned me to the end of the table. I jumped down. It seemed at that moment an awful lot of handsewers were in trouble with their knicker seams. My mate whipped a lid off a box and there was my going-away trousseau.

> two poplin bras
> two pairs of knickers
> two poplin nightdresses
> one pair of breeches
> one shirt-type blouse
> one slightly worn canary yellow sweater
> one pair of flat-heeled shoes
> one pair of wellington boots
> one brush
> one comb
> one flannel.

I knew it was all over. I was on my way out.

HELLO WORLD

'It's getting up steam. You'd better get in, Gale.'

She turned the handle, and opened the door. The window was down, and I leaned against it. I didn't know what to talk about, and I could see she was anxious to get away. 'You can go, if you like, Miss.' 'I'm supposed to wait till the train pulls out. But I can trust you. I expect you've had enough. Well, I'll say good-bye. My daughter will be needing me.' Her daughter was an invalid. She had been telling me all about her while walking down to the station. The steam hissed out again. She had already forgotten me. I didn't bother to call out. I'd never liked her. She had seemed so hard and unsympathetic with me and my mates.

Perhaps it had taken all the love she had to put up with her daughter.

I don't remember much about the journey. I kept repeating the name of the station to myself. Then the train hissed to a stop, and I stepped out on to the platform. There was the station porter, but no one else. I leaned against some baskets piled up on the platform. What's that noise? I peered through. Pigeons! I watched them for a moment, and then remembered where I was, and what for. Someone was calling me. I looked up and saw him. Beyond the level crossing, he was sat up in a horse and trap. I was disappointed somehow. They'd given me a different impression back there at the Borstal. I thought of what the girl had said . . . then I made for the stairs and was walking across the little bridge that took me over to his side of the track. I was well in it now. They had asked me 'Do you like horses?' Well, I like all animals; so I had said 'Yes.' But I was nervous as I climbed up into the trap. Besides, he looked different, not so elderly or so kind as he looked when they came to see me at the Borstal. Then he'd been bundled up because they'd come in on a motor bike. He'd had his cap on back to front and motoring goggles up on top of it. Perhaps I'd looked at the lady more than at him.

In a little while, we were trotting down the road to the village, and I was listening to the clop clop clop clop of the horse's feet and watching its wide bottom moving from side to side. Woa! We stopped outside of a house with a garden. 'Shan't be long. Hold the reins,' he said, 'I'm just popping into the post office.' He started up the garden path. 'Hey mister! You said you were going to the post office.' 'This is the post office.'

We were on a slope. The horse was moving backwards and forwards just a little bit, enough to scare the pants off me, and its hoofs were hitting the ground hard. I kept saying Woa! like he had, and thinking 'Bloody cheek!

Fancy leaving me sitting up here. I'm not staying up here,'
I thought to myself. He came out then, and I relaxed. I
was grinning. Fancy going up a garden path to the post
office. Nice idea, though.

He loved horses, told me this one was a chestnut mare.
Men touched their caps, and women said 'Good morning
sir.' We met a lady out riding. 'Hello there! How's the
hunt?' She talked all frightfully-frightfully, you know. We
turned down a narrow tarmac road with green grass sides,
and cut through a field where the sheep were, and all the
way along was an avenue of tall poplars. They are lovely, I
grant you that, but they look a bit condescending, especially
when there are two rows about a mile long. I wanted to
squirm. 'Ah!' he said, 'this we call Poplar Walk.' But I
had forgotten them. I was hunched forward on my seat
with excitement. There across another field was something
I was longing to be in again – the woods.

THE HOUSE ON THE HILL

I went upstairs to unpack my case. I sat on the bed and
looked round at the room. I liked it. It was an attic room,
but very big. The windows opened out, and let in plenty of
air. The ceiling sloped down low, and the door was small
and just fitted me. Plain white-washed walls. I left them
like that. A rush mat covered most of the floor, and the
floor-boards were stained and polished. A table by the bed
had a candlestick on it. I was disappointed. After lights out
at an early hour in Borstal, I had hoped for long hours of
reading.

I knelt up on my pillow and leaned out. The view was
magnificent. It looked a mass of greens, reds, and browns.
Surely I would be happy here. I heard a dog yap. I ran
down the narrow flight of stairs which led from my room,

rich brown oak stairs, highly polished. I thought 'I'm glad they aren't covered with anything.' I jumped the last two and ran along a landing and down another flight of stairs into the kitchen. A funny little mongrel was sat by the kitchen door.

I looked through the kitchen window. Unlimited space. A great big field with hills dotted over it. I couldn't see where it ended. I wanted to squeeze myself with excitement. 'Come on, dog.'

I turned the big iron ring in the oak door, and Victor – that was his name – darted through. Soon we were running over the brow of the hill, past the duck-pond. Victor's ears pricked up. 'Hey, none of that!' he seemed to grin. Then he bounded on again, and I ran flat out, determined he shouldn't beat me, but he did. I collapsed on the ground, and Victor's tongue was lolling out. I picked up a piece of wood and threw it as far as I could. He just lay there flopping his tail up and down. 'Go on, fetch it!'

But just then I heard voices, and held him still, and listened. People were laughing, and calling to each other in the next field. I knew what had been worrying me ever since I arrived. It was the loneliness. How could I bear it?

The voices made me feel easier. It meant I might make friends. Talk with people near my own age. I heard someone call. I looked over the top of the hill. A big man was striding towards us. Victor's ears pricked up again, and he was off yapping and jumping up at him. Victor had forgotten me. This was the master.

Chapter Twenty-three

I was watching a play on television. It was a satire on religion. I've often thought about religion. I've gone to some lengths to find out about it. I thought the people on the spot should know you must be nearer to heaven when you're dead, but it isn't so. I want to say to people, don't send for a priest just because you're dying; go peacefully.

I don't know much more than that at the moment. I suppose I haven't been so concerned with religion, but more with people who profess to being religious, and doing things because they were *called*, as they say. God save me and mine from these people! Now, God! I've had a few verbal battles with him – he doesn't scare me any more. When I think of Sunday school, and how they scared the life out of me with all their hell and damnation, and what I've called God to his face – I get the feeling he's not responsible for a lot of the words they give him credit for. I'm woke up every Sunday morning by an insistent Dong-Dong-Dong. Now who has the right to ring a bell like that just to call a handful to pray! Perhaps I would like it better if it had more than one note.

We must stop this farce of doing things for God, and start doing good in the name of humanity. And may I make a special plea to the Volunteers. Don't think too much. Go out, and just do. You had a wonderful chance and muffed it. I'm all for anybody while on holiday helping out in some way, but it makes me angry and sad when they can only think of themselves as experts who have something important to say – usually on telly. You may impress the uninitiated but you may be sure people like me are made very very angry.

I didn't want this book to be a saga of sadness, and believe me it isn't. I've been writing now for three hours against a background of music coming from Susan in a high squeaky voice. The carpet is covered in scouring powder, and she's taken over the housework. My cup is really brimming over. Don't let anybody feel sorry for me. The sun is beginning to break through, and my feet are itching to get out, and perhaps we'll go to the new river walk, perhaps we'll take a bus to the river Thames – I don't know yet. Sunday is Susan's day, so I will have to ask her.

My mother said, 'I can't listen to you all the time, Joan. I can't do it. There's your father's dinner to be got ready.' I was one of six children, and there was my mother as well, and she could only think and worry about my father. They still do it, some women, still only worry about their husbands. Kids can be sickly, disturbed, dirty, lousy even, and they have only one worry – the old man. What is it makes them like this? Is it simply fear? Perhaps these kind of women are too timid, and the men too hard. I know why I'm thinking like this. Susan has just tugged at my arm, and I had asked her not to talk for a while. Perhaps she's jealous that just lately I haven't had so much time to spare. She wanted to tell me about a real bird with a broken wing and this broke my train of thought. After she'd done the damage, she very kindly told me I could carry on writing my story. I'm laughing because I can't be a man just for a while and have my woman protect me from the children.

SEQUEL TO SUSAN'S SUNDAY

We were out and on the bus by four o'clock, Susan and me.

'Where do you want to go, Susan?' I said. 'Trafalgar Square.'

We wandered about among the pigeons. They always seem a bit tatty to me, and I can't bear it when they swoop down. Susan can't either; she generally drops the tin and makes a run for it. 'Now we'll go to the pictures, Mummy.' Very decided, my daughter is. But she loves the cartoon theatre, sits through it all twice. I just relax. She won't come out until she's ready, and we are our own boss.

We wandered up the Strand. Susan looks in all the shop windows, and just sits down on the pavement when she's tired. Her shoes come off too, and it's a bit disconcerting when people stare. Susan is sublimely unaware. I have to be ready to stop at any given point. For instance, there's the Old Curiosity Shop. We have to see that, and I lift her up to look in the middle window where the Victorian dolls are lying in their beds. She remembers not to shout, because I told her about St Philip's Hospital and the notice which said 'Quiet Please'.

Our last walk is through Victoria Embankment Gardens. Now of course the lights are the attraction, not the flowers. We crossed the road, and I sat her on the wall, and we relaxed for a while and took in the scene. 'Look Mummy. There's O and X and another O.' 'Yes love, that's OXO.' It was big red-light letters on a building. She's only four but seems as bright as a button.

'What will you have to eat, Susan?' 'I'll have bacon, sausage and egg, bread and butter, and a glass of orange.' I had tea. I was trying to economize. 'There, Mummy. Nothing left.' And she wiped up the last bit of egg with the last morsel of bread.

'Don't let me forget my purse, Susan. It's got every penny we possess in there.' 'I won't, lovie.' She calls me 'lovie'. Susan's nodding, but here we are. It's our stop. I was busy thinking of her, how tired she was. The lights are green – the bus is gone – and 'Mummy! Your purse! Have you got your purse?' I wanted to cry. 'Jim will get it, Mummy – we'll tell Auntie Bess, and she'll ask Jim to get it.'

Well, it's gone now, I expect. Jim did what he could – phoned the bus depot, talked with the bus inspector. But I don't suppose I'll get it back. Sometimes I think I must be a face. Everything happens to me.

Chapter Twenty-four

LITTLE WOMEN

I was reading *Little Women*, and waiting for an older girl to
call over the back gate. We worked at the uniform factory
together. She was a skilled worker and I was just a learner.
I kept hoping it wasn't time yet, but my mother seemed to
think I should be waiting with my beret on, ready to go.
'Get your head out of that book! Are you washed? Is your
hair combed?' She would be out in the scullery washing up
or poking things down in the copper or shovelling out the
hot coal to put it on the fire in the kitchen. They seemed
such heavy jobs. I wished she would let me stay at home
and help her. There seemed such a lot of jobs that needed
two people. Everything she did herself. No washing was
ever sent out. Boiler suits, trousers, right down to big white
sheets were hand-washed, and even then she seemed to be
always making or mending – so much work.

The girl called, and I very unwillingly put away my book.
It was a crisp but sunny wintry day, and my heart sank,
thinking of the whole afternoon in that dark factory. The
dust used to collect in big cobwebs of fluff, our hair would
be covered with a film of grey fluff, and I always itched.
The girls were always so cheerful. They enjoyed being there.
I'd thought that's how I would be, when some school
friends had described the job to me. That's why I had
kicked up such a row. You see, my Mum, bless her, had
thought factory work, and perhaps factory workers too,
were a little beneath us. It amazes me that she should have
thought they were any different but that's how it was. I
soon realized I was out of my depth, and very miserable.

Pat

The noise of the machines deafened me. The machines themselves frightened me. And I hadn't been brought up for the hard give and take of factory life. I know what I have always wanted to do, but on my terms – to work with children. I have so many ideas, so much I want to do for children who are withdrawn or deprived, but perhaps even now I will be able to do it. I identify myself with these kind of children, and I think they need people like that to work with them, as well as experts. I saw an instance of this with a teenage girl at a nursery group who, because she was still a small child in her mind, was able to forget everything round about her, and by her example another very withdrawn boy blossomed out and became a little person. I would have to be with people with whom I felt secure, so that I could forget everyone around me, and then I could do for them what I do with Susan. There is no Mummy when we are playing, or when we are out on our walkabouts. We are two people, and if I like being on a level with her I don't see that it matters. In fact it's why we get on so well. This is what teenagers are angry about now. But they make me a bit angry, because this is not their problem only; it was our problem when we were their age, and in spite of their moans, and unless they learn, it will be their children's problem. I seem to be doing some moaning myself. I don't mean to. I love teenagers and spend a lot of time with them. We don't seem to have any special status with each other. I'm just Pat to them. They may not always have been angels – they would be the last people to pretend they were – but they have a loyalty and great regard for each other, and I am astounded at the way one has already taken on the responsibility of a family man, and the fight he has put up in order to do so. It makes me happy when Susan and me go to tea on Sunday or call in for supper, and I get the feeling more and more that with a little bit of luck this could happen for Richi.

Bob is Richi's best mate, and since the arrival of Bob's baby boy, Richi is already taking his uncle status very seriously. It gives him something outside of prison to be interested in. He's demanding photos of the baby and handing out good advice. But that's Richi and me. Maybe we're so busy worrying about other people we forget to stop a minute and think of ourselves.

WHERE WAS MY DAD

'Don't go along the passage.' I had been playing hide-and-seek. It was eight o'clock, and I had just come in. My sister called me out to the scullery. 'Dad's in the front room with some policemen.' I know it was a secret. I wasn't supposed to tell anyone what she had just told me, but I flew into the kitchen to my mother and blurted it out. 'Why do they want my Dad?' My mother tried to hush it up. She said 'Drink your cocoa' and things like that like grown-ups do when they don't want to answer your questions. I couldn't let it rest. I undressed by the fire like I always did and leaned on the fireguard without any clothes on – I still do it now, lean in front of a fire without any clothes – before I slipped my long white winceyette nightdress over my head. 'Good night Mum.' I kissed her cheek – it always felt soft – and then instead of going straight up the stairs made a dart for the front room door and flung it open. They all looked up, and I was speechless. I don't know what I expected to find, but things looked very normal. I made to go out, but one of them called me back. I looked at my father. He said 'Go back to your mother', and something clicked. I knew I shouldn't stay, that they would use anything I might say against my father, and I pulled the door tight shut. I breathed a sigh of relief. The kitchen door was still shut, and I crept up the stairs to bed.

Pat

My big sisters came back home, and my dad was missing. I noticed him gone because I sat next to him at the table. He used to give me bits of his meat. I didn't connect it with the night before. I was too young to understand, or perhaps I couldn't imagine my father doing anything wrong, and at dinner-time I usually went into my own daydreams, so that the scraps of conversation are scanty, the words wafted into my consciousness but scrappily, just a word here and there. 'He hasn't regained consciousness . . . He didn't mean to hit him so hard . . . I've told him to stay away from him . . . Bloody fool, to be jealous after all these years . . . If he hadn't screamed out murder . . . Why ever did he say "I'll kill you! . . ."' That was all scraps of mealtime talk between my mother and my elder sister. I don't remember my father's return, how long he was away, but I remember this brother, my father's brother, who he had hit very hard and perhaps nearly killed, was really killed a year later on an underground railway in London. I found myself even then wondering where was my Dad? And then I forgot all about it until now.

JOAN'S SUNDAY

My mother was very strict on our going to church and Sunday school – but I loved Sundays. It was a lovely safe day for me and special things happened. We woke up to a special breakfast. Nothing seemed so rushed as it was on school days. My mother looked different, more relaxed, prettier, and in a nice clean special Sunday dress. After breakfast we stood at the copper and on top was a gas ring, and she would hold the curling tongs in the flame, then blow on them, twiddle them round, try them on a piece of paper, and I always wondered if they were cool enough, and then curl the side pieces of our hair so that they would fluff out and look pretty under our best Sunday hats. We would go to early church service specially for children, and then walk from church to our allotment garden to see our father. Most times he would be just packing his gardening tools away, and we would walk home with him, helping him carry the flowers or the fruit and vegetables. I loved the little garden he had made for us. It was walled in with loganberry bushes, and the fruit was big and so deep red in colour. I could never resist eating them and always bent right over my toes so as not to spurt the rich red juice down my dress. There was the tool shed with a seat in it in case it rained, and an archway of rambling roses which was the gateway to a little lawn and a nice wooden garden seat under two apple trees. I could never understand why my sisters bothered to knock down the eating apples with a stick when the cooking apples grew much lower and were just as juicy and sweet. Perhaps the cooking-apple tree could afford to let its fruit hang low since no one wanted to steal it. 'Hey! That's enough!' my Dad used to say, 'you won't eat your dinner.' But nothing could have stopped me. Rich red beef, cauliflower, roast potatoes, or perhaps there would be succulent young carrots, lovely sweet garden peas or tender runner beans, or broad beans. Even the herbs for the sauces were grown on the allotment. And he would proudly boast about it at the dinner-table. As roast was my favourite dinner and I felt so happy I could squirm with pleasure on that day, I was inclined to agree with him. Pudding was a speciality. It would depend on the season, but I loved them all. Gooseberries as big as gob-stoppers, sometimes cold or perhaps in a pie or suet pudding. No wonder it was such a peaceful day. We were all too full to do anything but sit round the fire or on the back porch if it was summertime. After the washing up my Mum would say, 'I'm going to lay down. Sit quiet now, till it's time for Sunday school.' Perhaps I had always been quiet too long, but somehow the peace was always broken by my having to leave the Sunday school class because of bad conduct. It depended very much on what I had on my sister whether she told on me. If I'd seen her kissing a boy or being a bit boisterous, I might get away with a threat of 'Next time I'll tell Mum.' I remember these days now with pleasure, and wish I hadn't locked the memory of them away.

I sat at Pat's kitchen table and we drank cups of tea.

'I was sitting here,' she said, 'writing patterns with my left hand' – she normally writes with her right – 'and then beginning to write just like someone learning to write but like a grown-up does – words like "because" . . . And I was sounding out the words as I was writing them . . . I think that when I started school they made me stop writing the grown-up way and do printing . . . and I was getting angry because some of the words I couldn't sound out. I made a little dot on the paper and out of it circles that came out and out and out, angry while I was doing it, and afterwards when I came to clear everything I found there was a hole in the paper there; I think that used to happen when he* asked me to tell him something or do something and I couldn't – something that happened, how I came to be there, if I could remember something, how I came to have swollen lips and couldn't see out of one eye.' I said 'Do you think you had been really physically knocked about, then?' 'Oh, yes. I think I actually did have a blow. I think the hospital wanted to write me off as backward anyway and the blow was immaterial. And he was fighting this . . . And then I found myself writing *Pierre Durant*.

'. . . I remember he was going off to be married, and being upset and crying. (I can't understand not seeing any other children in that place.) He said "I'll be away six months. I expect you'll still be here when I get back. But if

* The hospital doctor.

you're not, remember everything I told you." I remember a young doctor putting his head in at the door, looking at his watch, and saying, "Come on, Pierre." And then I remembered about his name.'

I said, would she like to go to Somerset House, and try to look up his marriage certificate. And would she like to find out about her husband's money. (She had told me her husband's grandfather made a will; he had bought his own son a farm; but in his will, he said his own farm, after his second wife's death, together with his houses and cottages, should be sold and the proceeds divided between his five grandchildren. Her husband was already in Friern when the will was proved, and the money was in probate. About five years ago, Pat said, she went to Somerset House with a social worker, looked up the will, and paid six shillings for a copy of it, but never went back to collect it. 'He's supposed to get eighteen shillings a week, and it was terrible seeing him in hospital like someone out of Belsen — what was the man spending eighteen shillings a week on? I'm not interested in money for myself but the residue was supposed to come to me, and it might help Richi.')

We went to Somerset House, and the will was just as Pat said. Not a word invented or misremembered.

But we couldn't find any record of the marriage of Pierre Durant, or any name like it. Of course he might have gone back to France to be married.

I wrote to the biggest hospital in the Swindon district to ask if they had records of a doctor named Pierre Durant being on their staff forty years ago, but they hadn't. It didn't matter. I said to Pat: 'Should we go back to Swindon?'

Chapter Twenty-five

So we took the train back to Swindon.

Pat could not say if the station had changed much because the only time she had ever seen it was when the train had paused there and her father had stepped in and pushed her back into the carriage. 'You're not coming home, my girl' – wasn't that what he had said? But once outside the station she recognized everything.

Everything was where she said it was. Even names over little shops were the same as thirty-five years ago, and the initials of the Great Western Railway shouted out everywhere, unaware they had been wiped out twenty years back.

Pat danced on ahead, skipping like a child, exclaiming. It was fantastic that after so long everything should still be the same, that even the war had raged only elsewhere and not touched Swindon. Surely a town so unaffected by change must have had a talent for it?

She took me everywhere, without hesitation. 'That was a fish-shop – Mr Todd ... there it is! And that was the butcher's, Mr Hopkins, yes, there! And that was a baker's – yes. And a tobacconist's – yes. All the same, all the same names still! That was where my Mum took me – that factory, you remember?' – we peered into the black window – 'still making the same ruddy uniforms! And that was where my Dad worked, making trains – look, the railway workshop! Yes, that's where we collected our tickets for the free outing for poor children. And that's the rec – and beyond there's where my Dad used to go for a drink. This club here's another place where my Dad used to drink, the working men's club. He used to bring a bottle of stout home. My Mum wouldn't go out for a drink, but she liked a drop of stout.

'Here's the market. This is where we used to get our meat. My Mum used to come here Saturday nights, eight o'clock, when they were auctioning the joints off cheap. And that was where we used to get bits of cloth. The man had two fingers on one hand. He used to hold the piece up, and slap it with this hand and say, "Five-and-six? Five bob? Four-and-six?" I used to think, "I don't know why he goes through all this rigmarole except that it gives me enter-tainment." I always knew he was going to come down to two bob and sell it for that, or he'd have had it left on his hands.

'There, that place, Wootton Bassett' – it was on a notice-board – 'that's where I took all those kids. I stood on the pavement and said "I'm walking to Wootton Bassett. Who wants to come?" And I collected a whole crowd of them. Their parents were going mad – they didn't know where they were.' She stopped a passer-by as we stood there. 'How far is it to Wootton Bassett?' she asked him. 'Seven miles,' he said. 'Seven miles! No wonder the other kids were half dead and crying! I wasn't. I can always walk miles. Ten, twenty . . . I'm still as bad. I pushed Susie right to Tower Hill from Hackney, with nappies and bottles.

'When I came round this corner, my Mum must have laid down a boundary, you know, 'cos I used to be terrified, trembling all over. I suppose she was afraid I'd meet boys.

'That was the pictures. Here it is. My aunt used to come and ask if she could take me to the silent pictures. They didn't talk, you know, it was written down, and of course I couldn't read so I didn't understand anything of what was going on.

'And then I went to the talkies. They were showing *Sign of the Cross*, and I fainted, and the first-aid people had to carry me out and get an ambulance. They were ever so pleased with themselves. It was exciting for them. They said "You'd better go home now, dear." And I said, "What, pay me money and not see it?" So they were angry. They said, "We've brought you round. If you faint again, you needn't expect us to do anything about it." So I went back in and scrabbled about on the floor in the dark for my toffees that I'd spilt, and saw the whole thing through.

'Look at the buses! You know, I never went on a bus. Fourteen years in the blooming place and I never went on a bus. My Mum never went on a bus, you know. She never went anywhere, only to her operatic thing once a week. She was too busy, cooking and washing and ironing and mending.

'That's where I had my first bought-for-me coat. My Mum used to unpick things and make them over and press them . . . And here's where I had a pair of bought-for-me shoes.'

We were in the main road. 'I was never allowed to walk this street in the evening. My Mum said this was where bad girls walked. Well, there was nowhere else for them to go.

'This was where my cousin lived. She was the local Beauty Queen. She had a nice face, and a nice bone structure. So did one of my sisters. It was for the Carnival. The Carnival was the big event of the year, and my sisters helped to make dresses for me and my other sisters, and the bicycles were decorated. Decorations! She was a proper royalist, my Mum – we had the Queen and the two little princesses over our bed.

'There's the railwaymen's clinic, where my Mum brought me when I fell and hurt my back. We went in this door. And over the road was the other clinic – there – where I went to have a tooth out, and we used to get medicine. Funny how they trusted you. I used to come home with those big blue bottles with the lines down them, marked *poison*, liniment for my Dad or something, and no one thought anything of it.

'That was the theatre across the road where I helped the magician, unbeknown to my Mum. This shop was where a girl I went to school with used to slip in and buy five Park Drive. She thought she was a right devil. Her Mum took in theatricals. That's how I got that job with the magician. Never dared tell my Mum, though. He made beer appear out of nothing, and we were supposed to stand there and then give it out to the audience. This girl, her sister was in the pay-box, and her mother used to take in variety artistes, and there was one act, a Chinese act, with long finger-nails and their faces made up yellow, and green lights, and they used to practise in the garden with high trellis work, and I used to peer through, and even without the make-up I was terrified, and I used to run away . . . come back, and watch them again. All the local boys used to come to the theatre, and I was terrified it would get round to my Mum.

'That's where everyone tied ropes round the Conservative candidate's car, and pulled him along. We always voted Conservative. I was very eager for him to get in – the kids got a free bun-fight. I remember he came out on the balcony there, and a crowd of Labourites came down the hill there and threw a brick, and it hit his wife. And my mother talked about "That Labour rabble!"'

'My sister used to belong to the Young Conservatives Club. I suppose that was how she got out. We weren't allowed to walk in the High Street, but I suppose she used to spend five minutes in the club, and the rest of the time in the street with the boys.'

Now we turned down an alleyway. 'This is where I used to play with Denny. There was sand here, and clay. Those two houses were there, and in one of them a woman coughed herself to death. I used to go up there, and along there, right up there, and a long walk after that, to a house where I worked for five bob a week, from about nine to four-thirty, slugging my guts out doing housework, and give it all to my Mum. She used to give me back sixpence. I couldn't wait to get home quickly enough. I was fourteen, then.

'Up all these passages, this is where I used to play. I used to walk all round these passages instead of going by the road. It was more exciting. You could look over people's walls. This was the wood-merchant's – look, it's a heating engineer's now – where we used to get sawdust for our guy. I used to rattle on his window when I went by, and he used to yell out "Just let me get my hands on you!" And this bit of wall is where I played ball. And this house I used to go past like this' – back against the alley, sidling – ''cos the woman here once chased a man with a hatchet. And this was our house here. Thirty-eight.'

Full stop. We were at the back of it, standing in an alley where corrugated roofs were weighted down with bricks. Before the day was out we would get round to the front of it and walk in through the front door. I had no doubts about this, but it might take time. In the meantime we needed a rest and refreshment. Swindon air was heady.

We made for a coffee-bar back in the town centre, and Pat said, 'You want to keep your strength up, you know – this is a real swinging town!' We drank coffee, and surreptitiously ate boiled eggs out of our bag, and sitting by the window watched the people plodding by, heads down in the rain. 'Haven't seen a mini-skirt yet, have you?' said Pat, laughing. She looked through the rain-slashed pane. 'I used to meet a girl on this corner every day. I think she worked in the hospital. She'd had a baby. You know how you meet people regularly, and after a bit you say hello? Well, one time she asked me to come up one evening and have a cup of tea with her and her mother. She lived with her mother.

And my brother found out, and he knew she'd had a baby, and he told my Mum, and there was murder. And Christ, all I'd done was to sit there and have a cup of tea, and her mother was there, a little grey-haired ordinary woman. Good job I carved my name with pride somewhere, I'd never have done it here, would I?

'Up there' – nodding through the window – 'was where the policeman had me. And that was the police station where they came to fetch me. My Mum used a word to me I'd never heard before or since. "Did you have connections?" she said. She was crying her eyes out. I didn't know what she meant. I'd never heard the word. She went on crying and sobbing, and in the end I thought, well, I don't know what connections are, but I'd better say no 'cos I can't stand her crying like this. So I said no. And she sank back on the settee, and said "Thank God, thank God!" ... I expect my Mum was one of those who said "The British police are wonderful." '

Pat got the second round of coffee. 'I just seen a coloured girl walking across the road. My Dad once brought a coloured man home. Must have been the first coloured man in Swindon. I don't know what came over him. He was very black, coal black. I was very little, and I couldn't make out why he didn't come clean when he washed because his hands, the palms of his hands, were white, but the rest of him wasn't. They had a wash together out in the scullery. And my mother's face! I thought, "My God, this must be a terrible thing!" "*Jesse!*" she said. Like that. I think drink unloosened him a bit and made him ready for devilment, nicely you know – unless he'd had too much, and then he was nasty.'

Outside, the huddled people of Swindon stared at their feet. But you could not blame them for the rain, or the wind that buffeted them.

'Look at them going by,' said Pat. 'The boys' shoes are

all down at heel, and over. Some of them look too big for them. Lots of them must be out of work. Nobody's clothes seem to fit, do you notice?'

A man in his early seventies crossed the window, respectably, aspiringly dressed, with shoes a good size too big. They would never fit him now.

'It's time to go back to your house, and go right in,' I said. 'Say you lived there once, and would like to see round again.'

So we went back. The front door had been painted red, and there was a key in the lock. We wondered who lived there. We knocked and rang. No answer. Pat called inside, 'Anyone at home?' Still no answer.

Across the road, a woman surveyed us. She looked a pleasant countrywoman, friendly, warm, and very ready to give and receive information. We crossed, and Pat said to her 'Have you lived here long?'

'Oh yes.'

'How long, then?'

'A good thirty years.' She must have just missed Pat.

Pat pointed back. 'Do you know who lives there now?'

'Why, old Mr and Mrs Townsend.'

Pat gasped, and turned her face away. I could hear her unspoken protest – *But there was a key in the lock!*

'They must be very old,' I said, covering her. 'They must be in their eighties, certainly.'

'Oh yes, they would be,' agreed the neighbour.

'Are they very frail now?' I asked. I meant, secretly, will they die of emotion if their daughter comes home after thirty-four years?

She laughed. 'No. Not at all.'

Pat was composed again. She asked about everyone by name now, eagerly, and the woman told her everything she asked, with friendly unself-conscious generosity, unquestioning . . . told her where that one was, and where that one was

(Grace, her youngest sister – the one she had written to from Borstal but who hadn't been allowed to see the letter – had a 'good job', supervisor at Woolworth's), and where Denny was and who had children now.

'And they're quite well, Mr and Mrs Townsend?' said Pat at last. 'You see . . . I'm their daughter.'

'Well!' said the neighbour. 'I never knew they had another daughter!'

'I don't want to give them a shock, turning up suddenly like this.'

But she laughed again. She seemed very sure of their impregnability. 'They're very strong,' she said. 'Mr Townsend does all the shopping himself.'

'Doesn't my Mum get about?'

'Well, I think it's just that she's a bit deaf. So she stays in now.'

'She's not ill or anything?'

'Oh no. Only a bit hard of hearing.'

'She never did go out much . . . How does she look?'

'Well, I haven't seen her for a while. Oh, three years it must be, because she doesn't go out now. But I'm sure she's perfectly fit, you know.'

'And my Dad, he's all right, is he?'

'Oh' – again the soft laugh – 'yes, he's all right. He's a very powerful man. He's generally home by now. He comes walking down the road with his stick about this time, or a bit earlier. He's very regular in his ways . . . Are you sure there was no one in? He's generally in at this time.'

'Well, we'll knock again,' said Pat, 'on our way to see Grace in Woolworth's. Maybe we'll come back later.'

So in passing we crossed the road again, more because the neighbour seemed to want us to, than anything – and called in, just once more. The call back riveted us. 'Come in!'

So there was someone in. Pat stared at me. Half over her

shoulder, she repeated back into the house, 'Can I come in, then?'

'Yes. Come inside!'

I lingered in the hallway, so I didn't hear her father say 'It's Joan', as Pat said he did. 'He must have spoken first,' she said in the train going back, because I'd have said "It's Pat", wouldn't I?' And I didn't see the expressions on their three faces, nor the muscles in their bodies as they stared at one another. When I followed in, her father and mother sat comfortably in two armchairs on either side of a banked-up fire, a huge powerful virile man, and a tiny rag doll of a woman with no bones or nerves or blood but with tight stuffing as good as new, and Pat danced between. That 'Come in' had gone to her head.

She went backwards and forwards between the two of them, hugging them, kissing them, smoothing their hair, stroking their cheeks. Her eyes were wet and she wiped her tears away on their shoulders, on their cheeks, their knees, laughing. She was not at all hysterical, only happy and delighted to be home, to be told to 'come in'. She couldn't stop touching them, feeling her skin, her identity, close to theirs. She kept jumping up, to examine something she remembered, and then was back holding them tight again; and in their first shock, they let her. 'Where's your picture, Dad? The picture of the soldier? It used to hang here. And there was a shelf here over the fire. But the fire's different. You've gone all posh and modern.'

She touched the walls, as if feeling for hidden panels, secret springs, almost listening. She ran her fingers over the furniture. She examined and exclaimed. 'There used to be an oven here ... and an oven there.' She flung herself down by her mother, and put her arms around her, her face against hers, gazing out through the window. Her mother was bewildered. 'Out there you used to do the washing, didn't you, Mum? And you remember when the curtains caught fire on that window, and you put them out with your hands?' She stroked her mother's hands and looked tenderly into her face. 'Do you, Mum? . . . And you remember those fire-things we bought you from Woolworth's, one Christmas, we all clubbed together . . .?'

Her mother said suddenly, 'I've still got the beads you all bought me, the string of beads. I've still kept it.' Perhaps the emphasis was on the 'all', not on 'you'; or perhaps Pat had nothing to do with the beads at all. 'Have you?' she said absently, not interested. Then, quickly again, 'We always bought Dad a pipe or a pouch from Woolworth's, didn't we? And –' she was on her feet again, interrupting herself – 'oh, look at the kitchen, the new kitchen! Aren't you posh! And a bathroom too, next door! Who made this for you?'

Her father took his pipe out of his mouth. He was enjoying himself. 'I did a bit myself,' he said. 'And then Jesse worked at it.' I guessed that was his son. They must both be Jesse.

'Isn't it lovely!' said Pat, gazing in. She came back into the living-room and knelt down beside her mother again. 'You used to cook so much, Mum. You were always working.'

'She still makes her dough-cakes,' put in her father.

'Do you, Mum?' She gazed out through the window again, as she knelt there. 'And that's where the dog had her puppies, and you called us out to name them, Dad . . . Can I go out there, can I go out in the yard?'

I watched the three faces in silence. I think the mother thought I was Pat's 'keeper' – a social worker, perhaps. When Pat had introduced me as her friend, the mother said with emphasized meaning, 'I am sure she is a good friend, a very good friend', as if she thought I kept Pat on bread and water. Now that Pat was out of the room, she said to me 'Would you care to partake of something?' but I politely refused; I didn't want to shift the focus. She talked to me about her other children, and her grandchildren, and their illnesses, and this made it easy for me to insert a question. 'Joan was very ill when she was little, wasn't she? What was the matter?' Her face had a groping look. I turned to the father. And he looked back to her. 'What was the matter with Joan when she was little?' he said. 'Wasn't she in hospital?'

Now she spoke quite definitely. 'No. She was never in hospital. She was never ill. Never.'

Mr Townsend gave a laugh. 'She'll remember soon. She'll come round to it.'

I said, 'Do *you* remember?'

There was a pause, and then he said, 'No. Since I had my black-out twelve months ago, names and dates are lost to me.'

Just then Pat came back, still dancing. She knelt by her father, her arms across his knees, her home-cropped head turned up to him like St Joan. I thought he was flattered. 'Was your leg always bad then, Dad?' she said with concern.

'Oh yes,' he said. He had been rubbing it. 'A long time back . . .' That must have been the liniment for his leg, in the lined blue bottles.

'What did you do to it, then? How did it happen, Dad?'

'Ah, it was in Ireland.'

'.What were you doing in Ireland?'

'After the war' – it was the Boer war – 'we were sent to Ireland. I was a captain. I was getting my feet out of the stirrups, and instead of taking both out I took this one out, and when he rolled over he rolled on top of me. I made it worse when I had my black-out.'

'You had a black-out, did you? When was this, then?'

'Oh, twelve months ago.'

She came back and sat by her mother. 'Why don't you

ever go out, Mum? The lady across the road says you don't
go out.'

'Well,' said her father, 'she's hard of hearing now.'

'But you could still go out,' Pat said to her.

'I don't want to go out,' said her mother. 'I'm happy at
home.'

'You never did want to go out, did you?' She stroked her
mother's face. 'You've got fatter. Your face is fatter. You
used to be so thin, terribly thin. I used to worry about you.'

'It's because she doesn't get about now,' said her father.
Perhaps he was afraid it might seem that she was self-
indulgent.

'I hope you look after her,' said Pat, still caressing her.
'. . . And what about you? Are you all right?'

'As long as I have my beer and my pipe,' he said deliberately, 'I'm all right.'

'I see you still can't control him,' Pat joked to her mother.
'He still gets his beer.'

'He's been a good father to you!' Her mother shot at her
like a flash.

Pat smiled. 'You are a prim upright little thing, aren't
you?'

Her father had an air of secret relish about him. An
unexpected pleasure had come his way, a joke almost, and
with a few beers inside him he was glowing in it. He had
had just enough to be happy; a few more and he might
have taken his stick and turned us both out; but as it was,
he relished having us there. But she, his wife, was beginning
to realize what had happened – that Pat had got in again.
The key in the door – was it there because she was deaf or
because he was a little bit drunk? And would it ever be
there again? We had taken her by surprise, so that she had
shown a little pleasure, a little reciprocity. But already she
was beginning to pull herself together and remember her
role in the family, even if she was eighty-five, and now she

began to pull away from Pat's arms and even slap at her hands a little with an inturned pursed-up irritation.

Pat sat back on her heels, and spoke across to her father. 'Do you remember you left the dog at the vet's to be put down, and he got away, half-drugged, and came staggering home to die?'

'Oh yes. Yes. That was Rollo, poor old Rollo. He was getting on, you know.'

'Or was it Mick? The one you called after Mick the Miller?'

'Yes. Yes.' He pondered a little, sucking at his pipe. 'That's when I was rearing the greyhounds. Yes, it was Mick. And Dinah I bred from Mick. We used to get the rabbits, I do remember. He was a good dog. Yes. I would just point – and he was away. And I do bet that do bring 'em back! Ah, we used to walk and walk!' His voice was slow and full and sometimes very West Country. He was power-ful and virile, and only his chest which mewed in the back-ground like a lost kitten reminded you he was eighty-seven. 'I used to go long walks with you sometimes,' said Pat wist-fully, but he didn't hear her.

Pat talked about her sisters, and her one brother. 'I was a year older than Grace, wasn't I?' She became a bit uncertain. 'Which was younger, then, Grace or me?'

Neither of them answered. Finally her mother said, 'I don't know.' And after a little more silence her father said, 'I don't know. Difficult to say . . .' He looked at his wife, but she gave nothing. 'We always talked of Grace as the baby . . .' he said.

Pat leaned on her mother's lap, chin on arms. 'Do you still love me?'

'Well . . . Everyone gets a certain amount of love . . .'

'Well, I love you!' Pat was pushing it.

'I hope you've learned your lesson!' There are all kinds of answers to 'I love you'.

Pat laughed. 'What lesson, Mum? What are you talking about?'

Her mother withdrew nothing, and got involved in nothing. 'Well, I hope you learned it, that's all.'

'Do you remember,' said Pat again, 'do you remember when I took all those children to Wootton Bassett?'

Her mother did not want it spoken of. And yet, there was a faint glimmer struggling to get through, of pride in one's child's wicked exploits that are what many people secretly save for themselves when they punish a child. But her righteousness won easily, and she was undivided. 'Oh dear,' she said. 'Oh dear. That was seven miles!' In anyone else, 'oh dear' would have signified helplessness, even amusement, but in her it was astonishingly unqualified disapproval.

'Are you glad I came?' said Pat, putting her arm round her again.

'Well . . . to a certain extent . . .' The old lady struggled after impersonal words.

Pat laughed. 'To a certain extent? Is that all?'

'Well! When you went to . . . to . . . that place . . . You didn't get in touch with us, did you! You could have written to us, couldn't you, Joan? You might have been dead for all we knew.' She righteously threw the ball back.

Pat looked astonished. 'But you wrote and said you didn't want to have anything more to do with me!'

'Oh!' The mother was shocked at such openness. 'Oh! I never did any such thing! Oh!'

Pat soothed her sadly. 'Never mind then, dear, never mind . . . And then I turn up like a new penny . . .'

'Well, I hope it *is* a new penny, Joan, I hope it *is* a new one!' She bobbed her tiny head vehemently.

Then the mother contributed her only 'do you remember?'. 'Do you remember the Sunday school plays?' she said.

'Oh, when I played . . . what was it? . . . the Virgin Mary . . .' She brushed it aside as a joke, and her mother didn't know how to take this. 'Do you remember the operas you used to go to? *New Moon*, and things like that?'

'Oh, yes.' This was very reluctant.

'Sing for me, then! Sing some of those songs you used to sing!'

'Oh. I can't do that.'

'All right, then. Sing me your favourite hymn – how did it go? – "The rugged cross . . ."'

'Oh no!'

Father took his pipe out of his mouth and said, 'Why don't you ask Joan if she'd like some tea?'

'I've already asked her friend . . .' A pause, a little too long. 'Would you like some, Joan?'

Pat seized on this. 'I'd love some, Mum!'

I said then I'd love to have some too, please. Father said 'Come on, Lily. Stir yourself. Take your feet out of those slippers.' This was the first time he had exerted himself against her. She got up with surprising ease – I had expected her to have difficulty – and walked like a much younger woman into the kitchen, while the old man said, with his only open sign of very slight hostility, 'She kicks me with those slippers of hers!' Perhaps he thought he was excusing his remark to her.

She came back carrying a very large heavy-weight tray. There wasn't much on it, but it looked very unwieldy for such an old and tiny person, though it didn't seem to worry her. She said to her husband, 'Plates!'

I suddenly realized this was the first time she had looked at him and spoken directly to him. Evidently she always spoke to him like this, for this powerful man got up and obediently took plates out of the cupboard. But she immediately gave me a slightly deprecating smile, as if she recalled this wasn't quite the way to speak in proper circles.

In the kitchen, moving about at the stove and the sink, away from us, she began singing. 'Hear Mum?' said Pat to me. She knelt by her father, laughing, 'Remember that song you used to sing, Dad? A rude song. Something about "The Good Ship . . ." ' She sang. ' "And where'er I go, I take my po, And a little bit of tissue paper!" '

'I didn't sing that! It was your Mum!' He was tickled.

'Mum! She never sang songs like that. She sang . . . "I'll see you again . . ." ' She floated about the living-room romantically, and out into the kitchen.

I heard her mother say, 'Are you married?' There was no delight in her when she asked this, no reaching out, just a coming to the point.

'Yes, Mum. I've a little girl of four.'

'What does your husband do, then?'

'He's in hospital. He's been there a long time.'

'Oh. Do you have to work, then?'

'Yes.'

'What do you work at?'

'Oh, different things.'

'Where's your little girl?'

'She's in a nursery. I should have brought her picture, but I didn't think of it . . . Can I see my old bedroom, Mum?'

'Yes, if you want to.' How reluctant she was. 'It's Grace's room now.'

Pat came back, rather quieter. Later she told me it was furnished with a very 'modern' bedroom suite, 'a long long dressing-table, bottles and creams and carpets and mirrors all over the place'. She was angry because the living-room that her mother spent her time in was dark and dingy.

But over the cup of tea Pat was still talkative. 'Do you still vote Conservative?'

'Oh yes. We've always voted Conservative,' said her

father. But the mother, mindful of a visitor, said primly, 'We mustn't discuss politics.'

'. . . And do you own this house now,' Pat asked, 'or do you pay rent for it?'

Her mother was not sure what stance to take. I could see Pat had always brought doubt into her life and had to pay for it. 'Well. We've bought this house several times over, all the rent we've paid.'

And father added helpfully, 'Well, we've been here fifty-six years.'

'So then Grace bought it for us. And she and her husband live upstairs. They've got their own flat there.'

(Going home in the train, Pat was to say, 'All those years paying for that house, and it still had to be bought. And they still vote Conservative.')

Pat was sitting again half at her mother's feet, half with her arms round her. 'You remember what you always called me? . . . Plain Joan. You remember why? Because you only gave me one name, and you gave all the others two. Why was that? Why did you?'

'Yes. Grace Amelia. Mona Winifred. Katherine Margaret. Jesse William . . . He's in Southsea now.' She was talking family details again. She had spoken their names with pride, but not vanity – a cheerless satisfaction is perhaps a better description She never did answer Pat's question.

'And you remember Auntie Flo? We went away to her once for Christmas. Do you remember? . . . And you didn't like it, love, did you?'

'She still had washing hung up in the room! She hadn't taken it down! And she didn't cut my cake! I was furious! Furious!'

'Yes. You were. I remember . . .' So there was another who had introduced doubt. Pat told me afterwards, 'My poor Aunt Flo. She had about fifteen kids. And after all

those years, forty years, my Mum still gets furious about
the washing hung in the room. She hated going, my Mum.
She worried so much about Christmas. Everything had to
be a certain way. It wasn't fun. I used to wish we never
had Christmas.'

But Dad said, with a laugh, 'And she had a cheap ham!'
It was difficult to say how far his contributions were for
playing along with his wife, or for stirring things up a bit
more, or for secretly laughing at her because he had had a
few drinks . . . perhaps all together. Certainly there was
this feeling that this powerful man had survived because he
had made an unspoken unassailable bargain. Some people,
many people, make certain alliances, like politicians' non-
aggression pacts, so that they can function. There is no
warmth in these pacts; they are alliances not friendships;
but sometimes there may be a certain grim relish in them –
this is the height they sometimes reach. But this unreproach-
ability, this keeping to the rules, is important to all the
players. One has to be able to say, quick as a flash, 'He's
been a good father to you!'

Now mother was recovering her equanimity, talking
impersonally about a granddaughter whose photograph
was on the sideboard. 'I've got a little girl,' said Pat again.
'She's four . . . And I've got a boy of twenty-two.'

'Have you? Why aren't you married, Joan? Where is
your husband? Are you a widow?'

'Well . . . a grass widow.' Pat was laughing it off.

'No. Joan! Joan! You should be married!'

'Mum, I *am* married. I told you. Eight years after I got
married, my husband got ill, and he's been in hospital ever
since. He was ill in the head.'

'Oh. I see,' doubtfully, easily reckoning up despite her
eighty-five years. 'That's sad.'

I caught Pat's eye and gestured to the clock. We had a
train to catch. Pat stood up, reluctantly.

Pat

'Is your boy at home?' said her father.

'No. He's away at the moment.' She picked up her bag. 'Well, we must go. I'll just have time to see Grace before she leaves work.'

With sudden astonishing power the mother said 'No! Joan, you will do nothing of the sort! No! No! You are a stranger to her! I won't have you going to her work! I don't want anyone to know our private affairs! Grace knows nothing about you!'

The father, still sitting in his chair, filled in the startled silence with a laugh, and then offered, 'Well, she'll be making up the money.'

'I see. All right, then.' Pat was sad and docile.

The father, still half laughing, said, 'She's got a very good job there. She's a supervisor. I think she and the manager run that place.' He was a man who knew more than he knew it was politic to say, and it amused him.

But the mother wouldn't leave it. It had to be made clear beyond a doubt. 'You are not to go! You are not to see Grace! Grace knows nothing about it!' She was definite, and angry, and remarkably strong. 'I don't want to talk about it! It's all in the past! I don't want to rake anything up again! It's all finished with!' She was very pursed-up, almost bursting.

Pat smiled and kissed her. 'She's a big girl now, Grace is,' she said gently. 'She's old enough, you know . . . But don't worry, my love, don't worry . . .'

As I took my jacket, Pat's mother said to me in an aside, one jailer to another, 'Joan can write to us. That will give me time to notify the family. This is a great shock. They must be warned.'

Mr Townsend followed us to the doorstep and waved till we were out of sight. Maybe the little woman stood behind

him, trying to see and wave too from behind his massive
frame, or maybe not; certainly he showed no signs of being
pushed or pulled at. He stood there apparently by a personal
and not easily assailable act of choice, enjoying himself, just
as he had enjoyed himself while we were there, savouring a
secret joke that his wife could not take from him. This one
might last him the rest of his life. Perhaps, as he said, his
beer and his pipe had saved him. But how many people
were sacrificed while he smiled secretly into his glass?

'You still care about them,' I said to Pat.

'I love them,' she said simply.

We did call at Woolworth's, on our way back to the
station, and looked for a supervisor who might have a long,
long dressing-table and bottles of perfumes and creams,
and we saw one who it might be. I said to Pat, 'Shall I
stand in the middle and shout out *Grace* very loud, and see
who turns round?' But Pat said no. Her mother's anger
had frightened her.

So we walked out into the pouring driving rain that I
suppose was beating people's heads down in other places
too and one should never be biased, into the High Street
where the biggest most massive building was the Baptist
Tabernacle; and nobody fitted their clothes. And we took a
train back to a place of unhypocritical violence, where all
the rejected live companionably together, with or without
luck.

APPENDIX

The rest of Pat's manuscript (see p. 30)

– Honest rogues more than dishonest Christians. So he ought to. I've met hundreds in my time. They are putting other people that might find some comfort in religion against it, simply by being such hypocrites themselves.

– Well I don't suppose you will ever truly turn Christian. You would need some miracle to convince you.

– I don't agree. Just let there be a stop to wars and more cures found for these terrible killer diseases, and stop the bestial cruelty done to children, and let people – all the ones that go to church – march in protest against these things. Then maybe I'll at least believe in their integrity and think there is something in it.

– What would you think of a world that could be developed on the moon for instance?

– I think it's a dead liberty! Put this one right first – all the money wasted on that and people still dying of cancer, and doctors and scientists waiting on hand-outs from benefactors before making the next step towards a cure. Besides, if there are people up there they should be left in peace. We haven't anything to boast about. I think people have got to find their own destinies, and if they go under, well, it's too bad, at least they feel like men and women, and not just bloody inferior. It's terrible to feel you are second-best all your life, and yet feel inside you something stirring.

– I think you sometimes think with your heart instead of thinking things out logically. After all, we can't afford to be so idealistic as that any more – but I sympathize with the way you feel, and I know you don't care whether it's a tramp or lord you speak to.

– No, I don't, because anyone can find someone in any walk of life who can talk about something of interest, and if it's something I didn't know before then it's interesting and I think to myself, 'There, I'm glad I spoke to him, or her, otherwise I might never have picked up that little gem of information.' Mind you, sometimes it's a disreputable old chap, and some people give me an odd look, but I don't worry.

– What about if you had an audience with the Queen?

– Oh, the Royals – well I've got nothing against them personally, and it's certainly better than dictatorship. There are far too many of them, and they have too much wealth. When you think of the terrible poverty still to be found in England, and the appalling housing problem, then it makes me very angry that a certain section of the community have so much.

– Well this was always the case – perhaps even more so in the past.

– Yes, I've read stories in very old books, they were so old the pages were brown and it seemed they would turn to dust in your hands when you touched them, and some of the things done in the name of Christianity and the laws of the land would make your hair stand on end.

– Yes, I've read such books, but it surprises me that you have a taste for very old works of art and books and things. In other ways you are so much a product of this generation, and knowing your age this fascinates me.

– What you mean is, I haven't grown up. No, not just that – other people of my age have grown up too fast. They feel old at forty. I get so mad at this. You would think they were eighty! Honestly, it's incredible – in twenty years almost, life has stopped, and I feel sad for them because there is so much still to see, still to do, if only people would get off their backsides and do it. I'm as poor as a church mouse and yet I could go out with just a couple of bob bus fare, and come home in the evening and feel I had conquered the world, and I would like everyone to share my happiness.

– Does Susan, your daughter, enjoy these trips?

– Yes, because I teach her to look and see, and now, even though she isn't yet four, she can appreciate even the first show of spring, and when we come out of our flat door she can look up at a wintry sun and say, 'Oh, what a beautiful day, Mummy!' Last Sunday it was raining cats and dogs. Now as I told you, I love it, but Susan just held her face up and stuck out her tongue to catch the spots, and her little face was just soaked with rain. But she said, 'I love the market when it rains, Mummy.' So you see weather or the state of it doesn't keep us a prisoner in the flat. Life is too unpredictable. It's no use saying we'll go out in the summer – who knows, the summer may not come. Grab it now, I say, no two springs are alike, no two summers, and we can walk the same streets, the same heath, the same park, and each time it can seem different – why? – because each time we are in a different mood, buds are budding a bit more, or the formation of the clouds is different, or it's maybe that there are different people around, or even no other people in sight. The main thing is mother and daughter are enjoying things together, and the more you show children of the wonders of growing, living things, the less they will want to keep up with the Joneses, and if their parents get out more with the children, the less they'll worry about the Joneses as well.

– Do you worry about keeping up with the Joneses?

– You must be joking! I couldn't afford to, and anyway I'm not the type. If I had a lot of money, it wouldn't change me because I have to feel free, and it would have to be just the same if I had money. I would spend it when I wanted and for what I wanted. When I say 'me' of course

I mean 'us', my children and myself – but I just expect you to understand that. I want to buy a record-player and records that appeal to *me*, and they will all be as different as chalk and cheese because that's how I am.

Susan finds it difficult to get off to sleep, and I think if she could lie in bed and listen to something like Brahms's Cradle Song, it might do the trick. She loves pop, and she is a great little dancer, it just comes naturally to her – but she loves classical music too, and it seems to relax her, and she sits and listens intently.

– Can you afford to buy new clothes?

– No, but as I wear what suits me it doesn't matter. Susan's lucky! Her little friend who is older loves to give things she was especially fond of to Susan, and she always looks smart.

– Would you be interested in writing for the theatre or television?

– Yes, I have wanted to do this for some time. I would write about people who are like me, I suppose, but it would be very funny in parts, because very sad people are also very funny people – and I know I could do it if I ever got the chance.

– Where do you get your acting ability from?

– I think my mother had it. If things had been different, I think my mother and I would have become great friends. I think she was a little afraid of my father – most women are. Anyway I've mimicked people ever since I can remember. Perhaps there is a bit of cruelty in it, especially if the people are pompous or too lah-di-dah, but I do it mostly when I'm by myself, or when I feel really relaxed in people's company.

– Do you find you can love other children, or can you only love your own?

– No, I suppose I love other children just as much. I help at a little nursery for deprived children, and I find myself almost wishing I could take one of them home, and I

192

honestly believe that I could love him or her every bit as much as I love Susan. With my own children, I think it is their love for me which is important, but I won't buy their love and I won't bargain for it. If it's there it will come – I'm very lucky to have had their love both times.

– Do you think you could live without it?

– That's a strange thing to ask me. I don't think I could even think about that without getting very, very disturbed. I don't mean that I only live for them – I live for myself as well – but they are such a part of that living, well, I suppose it's just a great sharing. You see, we don't hold anything back from each other. Take Johnnie, for instance – he didn't just love me as a mother, but as a person. Some women are perfect mothers – by that I mean perfect house-wives – but that's all. It's not enough for a boy or a girl, there must be a bond of friendship, a kind of 'no holds barred', so that mother and son or mother and daughter can each say, 'Well this is me, I try, and I love you', and know that the other, without perhaps even words, can feel that they are understood and the love for each other is still there.

– This is a wonderful thing, and I am very happy that you have it, and as I have told you many times, it is your biggest strength.

– Do you remember your younger sister?

– No, I can't remember her face or anything about her, and yet we were closest in age – there was less than a year between us. But I can't recall anything I did as being part of her.

– Does this worry you?

– No, I don't think anything that belongs to the past matters – at least, not as far as my life is concerned. I don't think it would help me to know things about my family.

– Do you perhaps say this in order to protect yourself?

– No. If I knew where they were now I would not get in touch with them.

– Why is it, do you think, that your family never got in touch with you?

– I think they were afraid of me, because they expected children both of the same parents to be identical. I think many parents are like this – ashamed or afraid of the child who seems different, who doesn't always conform. Perhaps they themselves feel guilty that they have this feeling, but it's often there – the feeling that they would almost wish to cast the child out.

– Do you mind being an outcast?

– Yes, and no. In a sense I revel in the freedom it gives me – and yet I feel very sad at the things I may have missed. I suppose every woman wants to show off her baby to grandmother, and deep down I wanted to do this. If I had gone home then, with my baby son, I suppose I would have been made welcome, and things would have been normal, but I could never bring myself to do this. I tried desperately to get on a train with Johnnie and go home, but I could never do it. Something always told me 'don't go, what's the use, nothing's changed'.

– Are you saying that you felt somehow that your life was still going to go wrong? – After all, you now had a baby son, and were respectably married – didn't you feel some security in all this?

– No. I can't explain, but I felt no joy, no security and no future. It was as if I was waiting for some awful tragedy to overtake me. I tried even to warn myself. Don't marry this man, I said – almost as if I was someone else. And with Johnnie too – I told myself, don't have this baby – just as if I saw all the things that would happen, all the heartache that was to follow.

– But if you felt this, why don't you believe that perhaps

194

it is possible to be forewarned by some power, beyond our own?

– I'm not arguing, and I agree it is possible – I just say that unless it is clear-cut, unless the person concerned is intelligent enough to understand or work it out, then there is no point in such goings on.

– Would you discuss these happenings with (we'll say) some worthy trusted person, who was perhaps interested in spiritualism, or even the supernatural?

– Well, both these words scare me a bit, and yet I've got too much cheek to let them stop me from finding out. If I thought I could learn something – yes, I would talk to someone who was beyond reproach.

– I think you should. I don't say that things would have worked out differently, but I think maybe there was some-one who could have guided you, told you what to let go of, what to hold on to. I think this was your right. I think people like you deserve some help, and I still think you deserve it. Be honest – are you any different now to what you were perhaps in your early teens?

– I hate to say this, but no, I'm not. I work hard trying to disguise it, because I suppose I sometimes feel a bit ashamed of it, as if it's a mentally backwardness – but it's not that. I'm able to think, feel, know right from wrong, care for my children, care what becomes of me – so I don't understand why I only feel it as a child would feel.

– It is with the mind of a child that you cope with an adult's problems? Do you really mean that?

– Yes, my mind is made up.

– What would induce you to become a communist?

– I certainly see it as a possibility of future power. Myself, I would not like to live under such a government, but that doesn't mean I am against communism for a country as a whole. I think people in this country are often very badly treated and very unfairly treated in the name of Socialism, so that it is perhaps more beneficial to have things done for the people by the people in the name of justice, rather than a welfare state which seems to be for the intelligent majority that know how to drain it dry.

– It is surprising to hear you discussing politics with such vehemence. Do you take any active role in politics?

– No. After all, my opinions aren't very important – only to myself, because it is a constant struggle to keep my head above water. But social or legal injustice infuriates me, and this country is riddled with it, and I have been in many ways affected by it. But I will not let it destroy me or my children, or take away my love of living, because in spite of one hell of a lousy life as a whole, living has brought me much joy.

– Are you a slap-happy kind of person deep down?

– Yes I think so, but tears are always so near the surface that I think I must be two people. I can't ever be stable, and I think I sometimes fool myself when I get too sad.

– You have no conception of what you are, have you? You sell yourself short almost unintentionally. You have a wonderfully happy nature, it is true, but to say as if with apology that the tears get in the way, is not true. Basically you are a very deep thinker, but somewhere, sometime, this has been crushed down, so that to show any deep feeling, except to me, is almost like laying bare your soul. I think because of what this man did to you as a child and because of the guilt you felt, you have been denying yourself the right to your true nature, as if you were doing penance for your childhood sin. I have a million questions to ask. I have still a lot to write about you. I want to know still what the future holds for you; whether your fear for Susan is based on fact, or perhaps fantasy, or simply the memory of a terrible nightmare that has stayed with you. I am very anxious to know how Johnnie comes out of his trouble –

this boy who has been in some ways almost a father to his own mother – and I will be looking for the story which is bottled up inside you, and which one day you will write. Will you promise to write it?

  – Yes, my mind is made up.

2

After I left the nursery group, Pat began to cope with it, sometimes completely on her own. Here are some extracts from the notes she began to keep:

This group was very hectic! The Joshi children were full of mischief and out for a lark. They took longer to settle down.

It is interesting to see how they enjoy music and movement. Mohan was enchanting dancing to Swan Lake. He is a stocky, well-built boy and yet moves with grace. He is perfectly relaxed when doing this and seems to glide into the rhythm of the music quite naturally.

Vinita enjoyed dressing up and Lindsay helped her with her head-dress and veil which was a lampshade and piece of curtain-net. We enacted a tiny play and Mohan held her train while she walked to the chair. He made a beautiful bow which incorporated the whole of his body. Vinita was proud but shy.

I think they are boisterous because they are very tense but should be quite active in the group when they have settled down. At the moment they are all one person's work. They have excellent table manners and eat everything. Mrs Joshi says Vinita never stops eating and this could well be that she burns up a lot of nervous energy. It is good to see her still sharing things with other children. She had a pleasing manner underneath her rather robustuous exterior.

Mary and Eileen Connolly spent the morning as usual in the wendy house. There was a serious discussion on the toy telephone with the doctor. She was asking him to call as her sister was sick. Mary also used biro and paper to make a grocery list. She is very anxious while playing in the house, and particularly while cooking. She is obsessed with the fact that hot fat might splash the children. I am not altogether sure she is enjoying it just as a game. It seems more likely she is living out her mother's worries and frustrations. She gets far too intense while playing house and becomes distressed very easily and cries a lot. I hope she will become interested in some other form of amusement besides the wendy house quite soon. Perhaps we can have a shop in the near future.

It is Mary's birthday next week and she will be having a little party with cake and candles. We will be giving a little party for each child on their birthday.

The mothers are gradually coming into the children's group more and Mrs Connolly sat in with the band and her own two children and seemed to enjoy it very much.

[There were seven Connollys – five children, two adults – living in one room.]

Five days later

Maureen Roper came to the basement at the unit. She had been in hospital for a few weeks and her children had been taken into care while she was away.

Helen, her caseworker, asked me if I could help. There was no official children's group due to half-term* but that didn't matter. The basement is well equipped for all emergencies and so we were able to use it on this occasion.

Maureen and the children felt at home because they normally come twice a week to the mothers' and children's group. This was a special day. Helen felt that Maureen should not be left to cope at home with the children. It was a wonderful success, so much so that this little family are coming again on Thursday.

We have a blackboard which covers one wall of the children's room. Kathleen and the children were quite absorbed with their drawings. Stephen is five and can draw quite exceptionally well, especially the heads of horses. He is a bright happy boy while at the unit; unfortunately at school this is not so.

I got out our small collection of band instruments and we had a session singing and playing pop songs and nursery rhymes. At first Maureen wasn't sure she could join in, but Helen got her

* The mothers all had other children at school, and on half-term holidays did not come to the unit.

started and gradually her face became less tense and she was even smiling and we were all relaxed and singing with gusto.

After this Maureen kept breaking into a little song. She looked apologetic and said 'Sorry Pat, but I'm enjoying myself so much!' This is the whole idea of the basement, to use it for enjoyment, and for when a mother is weighed down with a burden too heavy to carry; she can lay it down if only for a day and if she so fancies even herself become a child.

Maureen loves the free and easy atmosphere of the basement. 'We can do as we like, Pat,' she said to me in her soft Irish brogue. I like the feeling of that, and she did do as she liked. We played with toys and we talked as we played, and, more importantly, Maureen talked and I listened because I wanted to help Helen to help Maureen, and it was sad to hear her say, 'This is what I want to do. I want to play with toys.' How many people are desperately unhappy because they were never able to be a child and then are suddenly having to cope with a family of children? Perhaps like Maureen in very poor circumstances? Maureen of course loves her children very much but there must be this nagging worry within her, to be allowed some measure of childhood happiness herself though she is grown up and married and with four young children. They are all coming again on Thursday. I think we will all paint a big long mural for the children's group. Maureen and the children are looking forward to this. Something else we may be doing is reading children's books. Perhaps we'll have the puppets as well. It's anything goes for Maureen Roper and her wonderful little family and anything goes for me too, because Maureen's health and happiness is a matter of emergency. This is how we see the basement, as a place for all kinds of emergency.

Three Weeks Later

Today was a small group with four children between two and seven years, and also with Lindsay Foot who is at the crawling stage. It is interesting how very happy and content Lindsay is and quite able to play very happily and quite alone for long periods. Lindsay and her brother Kevin do not relate to each other so much now during their day at the children's group because Kevin, although only two years old, naturally wishes to join in the group activities and games with the other children. But there is still no sign of animosity between Kevin and his sister which apparently is worrying the mother when they are at home. We are very pleased that at least one day during the week this little boy is freed of any pangs of jealousy towards his sister. We are indeed happy that the child psychiatrist has noticed a big change in Kevin since coming to the group.

I was pleased too that because of our smaller numbers I was able to give of myself especially to the three little Ropers who needed me very much. They were very sad on arrival. Their mother had been taken from them once again due to a mental breakdown. This had happened for the second time in a matter of weeks . . . The children are delightful. Shirley, the eldest, rather serious with delicate features and a high intelligence. Julie has a round face, a roguish smile and beautiful red hair which frames her face, and blue eyes which really do match the blue of her coat. Stephen too is a very handsome little boy. His eyes are very dark brown. He has a strong personality and loves making things with clay. His drawings are full of fun and he is fond of using his hands. With a little help, when modelling he can be most original. During clay activities he is relaxed; he uses his imagination and while he is modelling the clay he has a smile on his face and a whimsical expression which tells me that for a little while at least he is very happy.

Elizabeth, Pat Brown's child, is three years; she was tired and wanted a cuddle. Julie had been talking to me but now she backed away. 'I don't love you any more, Pat,' she said to me. I asked her why not. She pointed to Elizabeth who was snuggled up to me. 'You're giving her a cuddle,' she burst out. There were tears in her eyes. I quickly sat on a nursery table, pulled both Julie and Elizabeth up close to me and sang them a lullaby; they both smiled and relaxed. It shows how desperately little Julie is in need of mother-love at this time and how glad I am that I see the need and can fulfil it while the mother is in hospital.

Mr Roper came to the unit to collect them. What a wonderful job as father and mother he is doing. The children's clothes are spotlessly clean, their faces shine with washing, and he cares so much that they should look nice. I was able to share my daughter's clothes among the girls when Mrs Roper was first ill and unable to help with washing, clothes which had been passed on to me from friends . . .

(From Leila Berg's notes:

The Roper children came to the basement the day they were going to be taken into care again. Pat watched little Julie going round and round and round the garden; she thought desperately what to do, and dashed home to get her one of Susie's dolls that Julie could take with her – 'I thought I must find one with hair that she could stroke' – and brought it back in time and gave it to her saying, 'It will be your very own. You will have it with you all the time you are in that nursery. No one will take it away. It will be your own baby doll.' Then what happened? Pat told me, 'My God, this was a place children only go to at a time of crisis. And that bloody woman, you know what she did? Just because Julie was rude to her, or was upset, or didn't do what she told her, she took that doll away and locked it up, and she's never seen it again. The kid's back now, and the bloody doll's still there, locked up!'

Stephen Roper, in the basement, played the drum, rhythmically, louder and louder, frighteningly deafeningly loud, chanting all the time 'My Mum's going to stick a knife in my Dad, my Mum's going to stick a knife in my Dad.' He is an obviously intelligent boy, with very great potentialities, but his teacher at school can do nothing with him, and only wants to throw him out – even though Helen, the Ropers' caseworker, has been down to the school and explained everything to her.

Mr Roper came out of prison the week Mrs Roper went back into mental hospital. He has cleaned the children up, and actually got them all back to school – they were always afraid to go to school because they never knew if their mother would still be there when they got back – but Stephen's teacher is not appreciative.)

3

THE VISIT

This morning is like no other morning. It is sweet and sour and I wake to the thought that today we visit Richi, as I lay there I could almost wish that it was over and I have a mad desire to sleep on it. Only as we prepare for the journey does the enthusiasm become apparent. I search madly for the visiting order which came with the last letter. It seems that the safe place is no longer where I put it and the tension mounts. There is an awful moment of panic and I see myself at the prison door begging to be let in and the tears of anger show themselves. I shout at Susie. I count my money again. Is there sufficient to pay for another three months' paper bill? The books. I should have parcelled them up. That new photograph taken of Susan. They must both be clearly labelled and left at the censor office. It's time we went but a friend is coming with us. Will she be on time? Only at the prison gate do we relax and as we hand in the order, we are glad sometimes for those few minutes before 'Visitors for . . .' is called. Susie needs the lavatory and so do I and so does my friend. I run in but there is a queue for the one lavatory.

The visiting hour is the same – the hour spent with my only son. It is a fantasy of unreality and yet as realistic as we can make it. Susan can make it easy and yet difficult. Only those serving time outside and inside the prison can understand. It is a code from the onset of emotional discipline and control. Richi has enough to contend with. I feel I must protect him from any added worries of my personal problems, but Richi strives hard to make the visit a happy one for us. Every moment is precious and every word is doubly so. Of course, we know we are hiding some problems from each other, and if we did not hide the agony of parting month after month we would both part more desolate than we already do. It is not easy and many times a man cries in the privacy of his cell. My son has seen the effect a bad visit can have on a man, has talked about it with me, it is good that he can feel for the agony of another.

When my son began this indeterminate sentence our visits were terrible. We sat tense, hardly daring to speak, each of us urging the other to find the right words, and the pain was unbearable! I was glad of the joke or brash remark that now and then broke the silence and which was only to hide the bewilderment to understand his position, that of life sentence for manslaughter but no date for release. I was unable, in the first few months, to give him any advice. I knew nothing of what had happened in the court-room. I had been called from the gallery and kept in a room until the trial was over. This was something else which bewildered my son. It still bewilders me! I could only believe what I was told by the barrister as the reason for the sentence and that was in order that he would not serve more than four to five years. I believed this urged my son to live with this date firmly fixed in his mind. Imagine my horror when the Assistant Governor told me that to tell him this was a foolish and dangerous thing to do.

I despair even now lest there should be nothing of his true self left. Every month as we talk I look into a young lined face and pray he will not give up, stagnate, become a cabbage. His sister suffers also, even now she is too overwhelmed to run into his arms, each time there is a shy hanging of her head, perhaps she too feels a certain distrust of a brother who 'works away' and never visits her at home! My son smiles at her. 'Hello, Susie, sit on my knee.' The shyness of two months' absence from each other gradually breaks down and finally she climbs up on to his knee, her little arms around his neck and as she smoothes his face she says 'Hello Richi, give me a kiss' and across the top of her head he will ask 'How are you, Mum?', but before we can talk Susan must have her share of this little hour and so because he makes no move toward the cigarette box, she will pull his face down level to her and ask him 'Don't you want a cigarette?' and is dismayed when he ruins her little joke by saying 'No thanks Sue, I've given up smoking.' But he takes it and her blue eyes match the mischief in his own as he attempts to light it just to please her. We both dread the time when we must explain where Richi is.

No visit is ever the same. I look back on the early visits with horror, the agonizing hopeless daily visits of his remand. Four long winter months, with only the honest opinion of picked prison staff to sustain me. These men lived in the hospital ward where Richi was. 'He's a man,' they said. 'He'll do his time well if he "gets a square deal". He tries hard to help the other lads.' Even more than that the thanks from other mothers whose sons were on remand for murder. Young boys who wished me to know how much Richi had tried (even in his own hour of peril) to help them.

Gradually the visits become easier. Richi does much to help himself and I smile my pleasure as just recently he told me about passing a bricklaying course, only to be slightly deflated when he grinned and assured me 'It was nothing, the wall was only three feet high', and along with his other activities he is taking 'English', perhaps to have a cockney accent is to be considered inarticulate or aggressive. Ask the youngsters who knew him once, or the elderly, they would describe him differently.

So time passes. He grows older. Time lays heavy on all three of us. The Governor tells me in a letter that he has worked through his own despair and reached decisions about himself and I am uplifted. The most important gift to one's self is self-awareness. I believe he has a good relationship with the prison staff. He has definitely a good relationship with other prisoners, all this where not to feel for anyone would seem the only way to survive and so month after month we step through the small gate into the prison. Another visit and yet another, but in all only seventy-two hours in the whole of six years and each time we sit in the same drab waiting room – waiting to be called. Susan pulls at my sleeve 'Mummy, when is Richi coming home?' and I tell her 'Soon, my darling', and she asks me 'Is it Christmas or spring when he will come?' and I have no words with which to answer her.

In the meantime, there are achievements. He has reached his peak as a boxer. My heart aches that he should reach it in prison. Yet he talks of it with pride and without malice, his professional peak is primarily the achievement and as he told me of it last month, he nods toward another table. 'Mum, that's my sparring partner.' I looked across the room at a broad-shouldered man of twenty-five or so and he smiles back a broad 'Hello'.

Richi's boxing style I am familiar with. I have watched it develop since he was six. The other man is an unknown quantity and I can only imagine it. But Richi does not hand out bouquets easily and when he uses the term 'terrific fighter', I know he has found a worthy opponent. Perhaps because of the desperate hope that life would still offer him a public bout, he has, during these long indefinite years, held on to his faith, and so he still gives up the freedom of a game of Saturday football in order to keep in training and runs five miles round the exercise yard in prison boots and in the unseen nod of each man for the other. The smile of a friend for a friend. There is respect. His sparring partner is black.

So another visit ends. The kindly, almost gruff few words at parting which hide the wealth of long good-byes are words enough. In the moments of despair like the 'Good-bye' one must escape from words of love. Instead there is a firm handshake and steady blue eyes from a son now head and shoulders above me tells me 'Take care of yourself.' As we go along the corridor we look back and hope for a final wave, but we have said our good-byes for another month. My son who has made himself immaculate in order to visit us at our table, to share what can only be one hour of family closeness, is walking away.